The
FINE ART
of
SMALL
TALK

The
FINE ART
of
SMALL
TALK

*How to Start a Conversation, Keep
It Going, Build Networking Skills—and
Leave a Positive Impression!*

Revised and Updated Edition

DEBRA FINE

hachette
BOOKS

New York

Hachette Go, an imprint of Hachette Books
Hachette Book Group
1290 Avenue of the Americas
New York, NY 10104
HachetteGo.com
Facebook.com/HachetteGo
Instagram.com/HachetteGo

Previously published October 2005
This edition: February 2023

Hachette Books is a division of Hachette Book Group, Inc.
The Hachette Go and Hachette Books name and logos are trademarks of Hachette Book Group, Inc.

The publisher is not responsible for websites (or their content) that are not owned by the publisher.

Print book interior design by Six Red Marbles

Library of Congress Control Number: 2022946304

ISBNs: 9780306831218 (hardcover); 9780306831225 (ebook)

Printed in the United States of America

LSC-C

Printing 1, 2022

To Jared Fine Holst and Sarah Fine Riggs, my inspiration and motivation. And the gentle wind beneath my wings, Steve Tilliss.

Contents

Preface

When I first got into the business of helping people cultivate conversation skills, I ran into a lot of skepticism. Invariably, executives would scoff at the idea of a housewife's trivial initiative to overcome boredom. Then I would get clandestine calls for assistance from folks with prestigious titles. People would construct elaborate covert operations to seek advice without actually asking for it, because they were embarrassed. I can appreciate that. In a previous life as a nerdy engineer, I was burdened with poor social skills and embarrassed by my own conversational ineptitude. Before I gave myself a remedial education in the Fine Art of Small Talk, I had been a poor communicator and a timid person for as long as I could recall.

As a girl I had been an overweight, reticent kid who sat invisible in the back of the class, often excluded because of my size. One of my most vivid memories of childhood is that of a birthday party for my third-grade classmate Rita. Every girl in my class was invited except for one other very overweight girl and me. That experience was so hurtful that I withdrew into a world of books. I had no idea how to make a friend or have a friend. Consequently, I never learned how to talk to my peers.

Naturally, when I got older, I selected a career without a high demand for conversation. I became an engineer—a perfect choice, since engineering tends to be highly technical and requires little chatting. I routinely made technical presentations or answered complex engineering questions without any trouble. All that was required was competence in my field. However, when I was sent to conferences or industry meetings, I was expected to mingle with colleagues. Network. Meet clients. I was filled with panic. I only knew one way to start a conversation. Without fail, I would ask every person I met, *What do you do?* After we exchanged career notes, the conversation invariably sputtered to an agonizing halt. I didn't know how to keep it going. I skipped every social function I could. The ones I couldn't, I'd arrive late, leave early, and, in between, pray that some other person with better skills and a kind heart would rescue me by initiating a conversation.

I struggled with the art of conversation throughout my tenure as an engineer. Then I took a break from my career to have my two children. In that interlude, I decided that I was weary of being overweight and self-conscious. I lost sixty-five pounds. My self-image improved. I wanted to have friends, to connect with the community, and to have fun. To do so, I knew that I would have to acquire better social skills. I took note of those who were successful at cultivating friendships and mingling in a crowd. I watched their techniques and timidly began to imitate them.

My motivation went into overdrive after my husband and I divorced. I realized that I'd have to start socializing if I wanted to meet anyone. Here I was approaching forty years of age, having been out of my field for a number of years, and needing to meet people. It was a daunting prospect, to say the least. But I realized that acquiring conversation skills wasn't rocket science. I convinced myself it couldn't be that tough or I wouldn't see so many people doing it so well. I made it my goal to figure out how to keep a conversation going for longer than five minutes.

One of my first experiments with small talk was a life-changing success. I went to happy hour at a local nightspot with a girlfriend. A man across the room began making eye contact with me. All night we kept exchanging glances, never speaking. My girlfriend prodded me. "Debra," she said, "just go over there and say something to him."

I replied, "Oh, I don't know. I don't have anything to say. Besides, if he wanted to meet me, he'd have come over by now."

But my girlfriend would not relent. She was so adamant that her challenge finally inspired me to go over and introduce myself to him. As I walked across the room, my heart pounded so loudly, I could hardly hear myself say hello to the man I now know as Rex. He pulled out a chair and said he was delighted to meet me. From that inauspicious beginning we began to date each other. A friendship developed, and I learned a lot about Rex. The most important thing I came to learn, though, was why Rex hadn't approached me first at the happy hour. I was certain that his reluctance was an unspoken commentary on some fault of mine. It had to be that I was too tall, that I still weighed too much, or that I just wasn't his type. I could not have been more wrong. It wasn't about me at all. It was about him. He was too shy to approach me.

I couldn't believe it. It really turned my thinking around. For the first time I understood that there were lots of talented, educated, wonderful people in the world who are incredibly shy. I realized that if my girlfriend hadn't insisted, and if I hadn't found my courage, I never would have met a man who became an integral part of my life. No, I didn't marry him, but he did become one of my closest friends.

That experience made me a convert to small talk. I finally understood what a great tool it could be for building rapport with people. I devoted myself to learning about it, practicing it, and helping others become good at it. I started my business, The Fine Art of Small Talk, and have been small talking my way around the country and world ever since. I have met countless fascinating people and made many friends. My life is now richly populated with a diversity of individuals who bring added meaning and depth to each of my days. Thanks to researching, learning, and living the networking skills you will read about in this book, I built a very successful worldwide speaking and training business.

My goal in writing this book is to offer what I've learned so that you, too, can reap the rewards that come from having a repertoire of conversation skills. The techniques, tips, and skills in this book are for everyone—not just nerds. I know salespeople who are wonderful at making formal presentations but who enter a networking event in a cold sweat. I've met teachers who can chat with students and colleagues but have no idea what to say to parents at school functions. Harried, yet happy, stay-at-home parents are a bundle of entertainment at a play group but walk away from a volunteer opportunity, board meeting, or church event feeling isolated and disconnected. I know one physician who closed his practice and joined an HMO because, despite his gift as a healer, he lacked the conversation skills and confidence to garner new referrals. The list goes on. Competent people from all walks of life need assistance to develop conversation skills.

Recently we have been met full force with virtual interactions, an even more challenging platform to connect than face-to-face. Thanks to video chats and Zoom meetings, lots of us are rusty at mingling and building rapport with other people in classroom settings or at industry conferences and social occasions.

This book will provide you those small-talk skills. Enhancing your conversational skills will no doubt improve your quality of life. I think you'll be surprised at the potency of small talk. It has an amazing ripple effect. Becoming a good conversationalist will bring new people into your network of friends and colleagues. You will find joy in the social events you used to dread, and you will create pathways and channels for new opportunities to present themselves. My dear friend Rex met an early death a couple of years ago in a car accident in Mexico. It is a reminder to me that the risk of engaging someone new in conversation pales in comparison to the risk of driving a car. Rex lived a lot in his forty-plus years. I am grateful that I ventured across the room to become a part of that short life.

Take a moment. Spend some time filling out the following "Winning at Small Talk" worksheet. If you answer yes to most, you are certainly on the right track. If you find yourself responding no to more than a few, it's time to get to work.

WINNING AT SMALL TALK

Please answer "yes" or "no" to the following questions:

1. I have joined or participated in at least one club or group activity in order to develop new business friendships or to meet new people this year.

   ☐ Yes   ☐ No

2. I'm conscious of "taking turns" in most conversations so that I can learn more about others and help them get to know me.

   ☐ Yes   ☐ No

3. In the past year, I have used my contacts to help at least two people find a new job, get a date, hook up with potential customers and clients, or I have provided information for other networking purposes.

   ☐ Yes   ☐ No

4. I attend either virtually or in person at least two functions a month where I can meet people, whether

in my profession/industry or who share a common interest.

☐ Yes ☐ No

5. If someone is friendly toward me, it is easy to be friendly back. However, I don't wait to make sure someone is friendly before I am friendly toward him or her.

☐ Yes ☐ No

6. When someone asks me *What's new?*, instead of saying *Not much*, I often talk about something exciting in my life.

☐ Yes ☐ No

7. At meetings, parties, job fairs, and such, I introduce myself to people I don't know and come away knowing the names of at least three new people.

☐ Yes ☐ No

8. During virtual meetings I jump in to say hello, not waiting to be formally introduced. Unless activity in

my office or personal circumstances do not allow for a live video, I do not go dark. I demonstrate positive body language, good eye contact, and genuine interest.

☐ Yes ☐ No

Well, how did you do? Once you master small talk, you are guaranteed to:

- Build business

- Make friends

- Improve networking skills

- Get dates

- Land jobs

All right—that's enough small talking. Let's get down to business!

The
FINE ART
of
SMALL
TALK

I

WHAT'S THE BIG DEAL ABOUT SMALL TALK?

You pull into the parking lot, turn off the engine, and sit for a minute dreading the next two hours. An important client has invited you to an open house in celebration of their new downtown office. You hate these things. You don't know what to say, you don't know anyone except the client, and you always feel like you're trying not to look lost; so you eat and drink more than you should, just to stay occupied. You must attend—that's a given— but you sink deeper into the front seat and agonize over how long you have to stay. Will dropping by for thirty minutes do the trick, or will you insult one of your best clients if you don't stay for the whole event? You search for excuses to get yourself out of there early. You could have someone page you at a specified time with a supposed emergency; perhaps one of the kids has a big game; or maybe you'll just allow your anxiety to carry you right into an illness.

Casual conversation happens at least a dozen times a day—on the way into the office, picking up your daughter from soccer practice, waiting for a class to begin, riding the elevator with a colleague, fielding a phone call from your mother-in-law, during a video chat, attending an industry meeting, taking a client to lunch, going to a job interview—the list is endless! Yet for some of us, these demands for small talk don't ever make small talk any easier. If anything, such encounters increase anxiety and cause some people to dread social events, business lunches, Zoom happy hours, and chance encounters with neighbors. Unfortunately, in our preoccupation with our own discomfort, our neighbors, acquaintances, and associates label us distant, cold, and reserved.

Remember Thornton Wilder's play *Our Town*? On the morning of his son's wedding, Frank Gibbs, the neighborly physician, confesses to his wife that his chief concern in the early days of their own marriage was how to make small talk with his bride. "I was afraid," he tells her, "we wouldn't have material for conversation more'n'd last us a few weeks." It seems acquiring small-talk skills is not exclusively a modern-day quest.

If your conversations evaporate almost as soon as they've begun, or if you're a reluctant participant at social and business get-togethers, you've come to the right place. This book will help you acquire the conversation skills you need to feel confident and poised in any situation. If you practice the simple techniques revealed here, you'll put your conversational demons behind you. You will learn how to:

- Engage any individual in a meaningful dialogue

- Resuscitate a dying conversation

- Transition into new topics

- Feel more at ease at networking events, parties, and receptions

- Manage awkward and uncomfortable conversations

- Make the most of virtual meetings and video chats

- Develop business friendships

- Step out of a conversation with grace.

GETTING TO THE BIG STUFF

Small talk has a bad rap as the lowly stepchild of *real conversation*, yet it serves an extremely important function. Without it, you rarely *get* to the *real conversation*. Small talk is the icebreaker that clears the way for more intimate conversation, laying the foundation for a stronger relationship. I believe small talk is the appetizer for any relationship. Whether business, social, or romantic, a relationship either begins with small talk then develops into something bigger, or it starts with bigger talk—a sales call or negotiation, a first date, a weight training— then thanks to small talk develops into something more meaningful and of value. Without small talk, rapport is not established and no potentially long-lasting connection is made. People who excel at small talk are experts at making others feel included, valued, and comfortable. And that goes a long way toward furthering a business relationship, closing a deal, opening the door for romance, or making a friend.

The good news about conversation skills is that anyone can learn them. Don't be fooled into thinking that all those other people you see who are smiling and happily mingling come by it naturally. Sure, some are natural-born talkers born with the gift of gab, but most have had to work at it. They've practiced, attended seminars, hired personal coaches, and read books. You don't think so? Trust me, I know. I used to be a geeky, introverted engineer—no one has worse skills than I once did. I became a pro by learning the skills and then practicing them. It's that simple.

The first step is to let go of the idea that we are all somehow supposed to know how to converse with strangers and acquaintances. It's simply not true. We are not taught how to do it, nor is there some biological mechanism that instinctively takes over when we find ourselves in a conversational quandary.

Mark McCormack, an attorney from Cleveland who founded one of the first sports management firms in the United States, once said, "All things being equal, people will buy from a friend. All things being not quite so equal, people will still buy from a friend." The bottom line: It's to your benefit to cultivate friendships, not just collect business cards.

The art of conversation is poised to enjoy a revival. Almost forty years ago John Naisbitt, in his book *Megatrends*, spoke to a future world focused on high tech yet longing for high touch. This high-tech world would place us farther away from our nuclear families, communicating with our colleagues and friends via faxes, emails, and cell phones rather than face-to-face. Not to mention Zoom happy hours, FaceTime, and WebEx meetings, which he could not have imagined. Driving in and out of our homes via the garage-door opener without any interaction with our neighbors, up and down elevators and on subways with masks on. Our new way of living, working, and commuting would create a void of connection with others.

Today we find ourselves exactly as Naisbitt forecasted—isolated in our niche, cubicle, or lifestyle. Membership in civic, religious, and business associations and organizations has declined because we have lost the ability to connect. Yet because of the events of September 11, 2001, not only do we Americans share a common experience of great magnitude, but now more than ever we long to communicate with each other about terrorism, war, and sometimes anything but terrorism and war. When a pilot has to instruct his passengers departing Denver International Airport on the weekend following September 11 to introduce themselves and learn about each other, then we have truly lost the art of conversation. It has become our custom to be so respectful of each other's space—or instead, so fearful of rejection—that we no longer know how to begin a conversation with strangers, let alone keep one going. Yet because of the longing for high touch, combined with the need for reaching out, the art of conversation will bloom.

We become better conversationalists when we employ two primary objectives. Number one: *Take the risk*. It is up to us to *take the risk* of starting a conversation with a stranger. We cannot hope that others will approach us; instead, even if we are shy, it is up to us to make the first move. We all fear rejection at some level. Just remind yourself that there are more dire consequences in life than a rejection by someone at a networking event, singles function, back-to-school night, or association meeting. Number two: *Assume the burden*. It is up to each and every one of us to *assume the burden* of conversation. It is our responsibility to come up with topics to discuss; it is up to us to remember people's names and to introduce them to others; it is up to us to relieve the awkward moments or fill the pregnant pause. Most of us hope others will assume these tasks. It is up to us to assume the burden of other people's comfort. If others are comfortable in our presence, then they will feel good about doing business or socializing with us.

TALK IS CHEAP . . . BUT VERY VALUABLE

Small talk is essential to creating and enriching business relationships. Always begin and end your business conversation with small talk to humanize the relationship. Investors choose financial planners as much for their ability to make them feel secure and comfortable as they do for their financial savvy. How important is your physician's bedside manner to you? Hairstylists are the consummate conversationalists. They understand that no woman will spend the better part of an hour or more sitting in a chair at the mercy of someone with a sharp instrument unless she feels comfortable!

In an indirect but very important way, small talk relates to how businesses and individuals spend money. In general, people and organizations spend money for two reasons:

- **To solve a problem or fill a need.** Think about it. You dash into a fast-food restaurant for lunch so you can spare yourself from packing leftovers. You hire a babysitter so you can escape for an evening out. You pay a lawn-care company to cut your grass so you can enjoy more free time and fewer allergy symptoms. You subcontract social media to relieve other staff of this duty.

- **To gain good, positive feelings.** My neighbor
  Susan continues banking with the same institution
  even though another bank in our neighborhood
  offers a better free-checking deal—because she
  likes the people. My friend Vince moved to the
  opposite side of town and still drives back to
  the old neighborhood to take his dog to the vet.
  Although he and the vet do not socialize together,
  he can't imagine going anywhere else. He likes that
  particular vet.

A good conversationalist frequently evokes the positive feelings that people long to have, and the reality is that buyers' choices about where to spend their money are influenced by the presence or absence of rapport. Small talk is a big deal because it is integral to establishing rapport. Parents and teachers visit before a conference to create a bond. Mortgage brokers chat with referral sources like title companies and Realtors to strengthen the relationship and garner business. Even a minimal amount of pleasant small talk will make prospective customers remember you better than they remember your competitor.

It's a tough and fast world. The news media provides more bad news than good. People appreciate a conversation in which they feel acknowledged, heard, and significant. While it's understood that people seek these benefits in conversations with friends as well as spouses and partners, it's also true that people choose to buy goods and services from individuals perceived as warm, friendly, and caring. From the senior executive of a large corporation selecting a supplier, to a parent picking up a few groceries, to the account executive calling a courier—buying decisions are all influenced by the rapport that has been established with the other party. Research holds that many of us vote for candidates for the same reason, good feelings, whether or not they are the most qualified candidate.

GARNER BIG GAINS WITH A LITTLE TALKING

Effective managers use small talk at the front end of a meeting to set the tone for discussion and to create a bridge to more meaningful, and perhaps difficult, dialogue. Casual conversation and informal icebreakers offer opportunities to build rapport, create a cohesive team, and increase the chances of success.

By developing your conversation skills, you can even improve communication with your children. You'll recognize the most repeated question in parenting—*How was school?*—as a conversation killer. You can avoid the usual one-word response—*Fine*—and instead create a dialogue. Imagine, you may actually gain insight into what they're learning and who their friends are!

Small talk is no small thing. It's a valuable personal and professional thread that connects people. Appreciating the power of small talk is the first step. By recognizing its value, you'll be more inclined to acquire the skills. If you thought small talk was all about becoming a smooth-talking used-car salesperson, you were mistaken. Small talk is the verbal equivalent of that first domino: It starts a chain reaction with all kinds of implications for your life.

This book is filled with techniques and hints to give you the skills to enjoy the perks of quality conversation. You won't necessarily decide that you love networking events, first dates, Zoom meetings, or cocktail parties, but you will have the skills to be successful at them. Like me, you may still prefer to stay at home with a good book rather than attend an event where you don't know anyone. There's no denying that it takes effort to mingle at an open house when the room is full of strangers. However, there's also no denying that there are plenty of events we're expected to attend. So it makes sense to maximize your opportunities, and improved conversation skills will do just that. By the time you finish this book, you'll have the information and resources at your disposal to make you a successful conversationalist at any function. Improving your conversation skills can enhance your leadership abilities, reduce your anxiety in social situations, boost your confidence, lead you to new friendships, and more. Before you know it, you might actually enjoy making small talk!

2

GET OVER YOUR MOM'S GOOD INTENTIONS

It's no wonder so many of us lack adequate conversation skills. Some of our oldest memories still haunt and influence us as adults. Because of our earliest training, we are predisposed to refrain from initiating a conversation. When we were impressionable toddlers, our parents taught us:

- Don't talk to strangers.

- Wait to be properly introduced.

- Silence is golden.

- Good things come to those who wait.

Those messages served us well as kids; the advice helped ensure our safety and taught us manners. But now, as adults, our safety isn't at stake with every new person we meet! And by now our manners are well established. The time has come to replace those old messages with more relevant advice. Here it is.

IN SAFE SITUATIONS, MAKE IT A POINT TO TALK TO STRANGERS

To expand your circle of friends and colleagues, you must start engaging strangers and acquaintances in conversation. There is no other way. Strangers have the potential to become good friends, long-term clients, valued associates, and bridges to new experiences and other people. Start thinking of strangers as people who can bring new dimensions to your life, not as persons to be feared.

INTRODUCE YOURSELF

When was the last time someone properly introduced you to another person? The truth is that the host of a gathering rarely takes the time to do so in a meaningful way. You've been to this kind of event. You go to a holiday open house hosted by an important client. The client greets you, takes your coat, visits for a minute, and shows you to the food. Your client departs to greet another guest, and you are left standing next to the shrimp cocktail, not knowing a single person in the room. If you wait for the host to come back and properly introduce you to some of the other guests, chances are your only new encounter will be with the shrimp.

Times have changed. People expect you to mingle on your own, introduce yourself, and take the initiative to get acquainted. As Babe Ruth said, "Don't let the fear of striking out get in your way." Remember, even your closest confidante was once a stranger. Take the risk. Walk up to someone and introduce yourself. Extend your hand, make eye contact, and smile saying, *Hello. My name is Deb Fine. It's nice to meet you.* Be the first to greet others as they arrive on the video chat for your monthly board meeting, *Great to see you, Hadley, how's your summer been?* If you are a member of an association, chamber of commerce, fraternity or sorority, church or synagogue, you are probably aware of these organizations' constant challenge of retaining membership. We join such organizations seeking out fellowship; we often leave or quit because we don't find it. Instead, we perceive others as members of groups or cliques that won't let us join.

I think most of us can relate to the following poem, author unknown:

Thoughts from a New Member

I see you at the meetings,
but you never say hello.

You're busy all the time you're there
with those you really know.

I sit among the members,
yet I'm a lonely gal.

The new ones feel as strange as I;
the old ones pass us by.

Darn it, you folks urged us to join
and talked of fellowship,

You could just cross the room, you know,
but you never make the trip.

Can't you just nod your head and smile
or stop and shake a hand,

Then go sit among your friends?
Now that I'd understand.

I'll be at your next meeting,
and hope that you will spend

The time to introduce yourself,
I joined to be your friend.

At your next opportunity to spend time at a reception, coffee break, hospitality suite, or wedding, look around the room. Find that approachable person and include him or her in conversation. Chances are, that person is feeling as alone as you are.

SILENCE IS IMPOLITE

Spare yourself some pain and forget the adage that silence is golden. I first recognized the downside of silence while I was working as an engineer, side by side with a peer who had the same academic credentials, tenure, and work quality. We were considered equals in every sense of the word. However, my colleague was outgoing and conversational. Staff members in marketing, human resources, and quality control knew her name, as did executives at corporate headquarters. Our immediate supervisor noticed her and commented frequently on her work. When the time came for a promotion, she got it and I didn't. I simply wasn't as visible because I was so silent.

I later learned another costly lesson about silence. My friend Johnnie, a regional director with a Fortune 100 company, dragged me to all her company functions. Her boss, Bob, a senior vice president, attended these functions, too. I admired his poise and grace as he easily conversed with everyone. Bob's self-confidence intimidated me so much that I rarely talked with him, despite my respect for him. Even when he approached me, I was too nervous to say much.

When I moved into engineering sales, I called up Bob to reintroduce myself and promote my employer's services. Before I could even finish introducing myself, Bob blasted me, saying, "I can't believe that you're calling me. We've been at the same parties a dozen times, and you've ignored me at every one. You're the biggest snob I know. I have no interest in buying anything from you." Needless to say, I was stunned and horrified by his reaction. It had never occurred to me that shyness could be mistaken for arrogance. While shyness and arrogance are worlds apart, the visible manifestation of each can appear the same. People generally do not give others the benefit of the doubt in this regard. Don't risk being taken as haughty or pretentious by keeping silent; it can cost you dearly. Start small talking and let others see your personality. You know how much you appreciate the efforts others put forth in conversation. Make the same effort. Contrary to what your elders taught you, silence is not golden.

GOOD THINGS COME TO THOSE WHO GO GET THEM!

Waiting will net you a bunch of lost time. You have to take the initiative. Don't spend another minute thinking that if you just keep waiting, interesting people will introduce themselves. It's never going to happen. Out of habit, and to make things easy on ourselves, we seek out someone we know—a colleague, a friend, a client, even a competitor. We are comfortable with these people because they attend the same functions, know the same jargon, and are trying to reach the same decision-makers. We end up paying eighty dollars to attend an event and then seek out people we already know because it's less threatening. Yet the purpose of the event was to make new contacts.

The benefits of acquainting ourselves with fellow parents at back-to-school night or extracurricular activities are clear. We forge bonds with parents to better keep up with and understand what is going on with our children.

If ever there was a place you'd expect people to mingle, it's a singles event. Yet they are notorious for attracting wallflowers. Most people at singles events—including myself in a former life—spend most of their time uncomfortably waiting around and scanning the crowd for a friend. When a friend appears, they immediately spend the evening hanging out together. If they wanted to be with each other, why didn't they just go out on a date? If they don't want to date each other, what are they doing spending the evening together? They're talking! Yes, talking—it's easy, comfortable, and safe. It is, however, no way to meet someone new and spark a romance! The same holds true for dating apps. Sure, there is a lot of rejection. But don't give up, reach out first. Think like NBA superstar Michael Jordan: "I've missed more than 9,000 shots in my career. I've lost almost 300 games. Twenty-six times, I've been trusted to take the game-winning shot and missed. I've failed over and over and over again in my life. And that is why I succeed."

Good things come to those who take action and start creating good things. American movie star, commentator, and folk legend Will Rogers nailed it when he said, "Go out on a limb. That's where all the fruit is." Although it might be scary to climb out from the safety of the trunk, you'll rarely pluck the sweet fruit by waiting there.

IT'S UP TO YOU TO START A CONVERSATION

Do you know the biggest social fear in America? It's public speaking. And do you know the second? It's fear of starting a conversation with a stranger. So remember when you walk into a luncheon or a cocktail party, most people there are scared to death to talk to you. Fear of rejection keeps many of us from risking conversation, but the probability of rejection is actually quite small. In the unlikely event that your efforts are unappreciated, remember that it's doubtful you'll ever see that person again. You will be the hero if you start the conversation. You will gain stature, respect, and rapport if you can get the conversation going.

Almost always, people will embrace your efforts and appreciate your leadership and friendship.

IT'S UP TO YOU TO ASSUME THE BURDEN OF CONVERSATION

If you generally wait for someone else to take the initiative in a conversation, you have been self-centered. It's true! You have allowed your own comfort to take precedence over every other person's. You haven't been doing your fair share of the work. If you've largely ignored your conversational responsibilities, it's time to take ownership. You cannot rely on the other person to carry the conversation for you—a monologue is a chore and seldom very interesting. Furthermore, one-word answers to questions do not count as shouldering your share of the burden.

The first step in becoming a great conversationalist is becoming invested in the conversation and actively working to help the other person feel comfortable. Take a look at the list of icebreaker questions that follow and make a commitment to use at least four of them in your next conversation. If you're afraid you won't remember them, enter them into your device or write them down, put them in your pocket, and refer to them before you to go into the event or attend a video meeting. If you go blank while you're there, excuse yourself for a moment and walk into the restroom to take a peek at your list. If you are at your desk, no excuses to go blank. The most famous and worn-out icebreaker is that age-old question *What do you do for a living?* It's so standard that it didn't make the icebreaker list. Here are some other ways to begin a conversation that will provide a refreshing diversion from shoptalk. You'll never ask them all, just the ones that seem appropriate for the particular conversation and time. And be prepared to reciprocate, since your conversation partner is likely to return whatever questions you pose.

BUSINESS ICEBREAKERS

1. Describe a typical day on the job.
2. How did you come up with this idea?
3. What got you started in this industry/area of practice?
4. What got you interested in marketing/research/ teaching?
5. What do you enjoy most about your profession?
6. What separates you and your firm from your competition?
7. Why does your company _____?

8. Describe some of the challenges of your profession.

9. What do you see as the coming trends in your business?

10. What ways have you found to be most effective for promoting your business?

11. Describe your most important work experience.

12. What advice would you give someone just starting in your business?

13. What one thing would you do if you knew you could not fail?

14. What significant changes have you seen take place in your business since your start?

15. Describe the strangest incident you've experienced in your business.

16. What was the best job you ever had? What was the worst?

17. What's the most difficult part of your job?

18. How has social media impacted your work/profession?

19. Do you know someone who can help me _____?

20. Describe how the economy/election/summer impacts your work.

An additional great piece of advice comes from Lee McIntire, former CEO and president of CH2M Hill (now a part of

Jacobs Engineering Group). Consider McIntire's favorite ice-breaker and use it for your own: "One question I have found that keeps the conversation going, creates interesting stories, and is nurturing is: 'You are obviously successful—do you remember your big or significant break?'"

I play with this a bit to make it feel authentic for me. I ask other professionals: *What is the number one ingredient you attribute your success to?*—a great way to learn from others while at the same time enjoying a more in-depth conversation. As we head to more generic icebreakers, this same question can be used for social interactions when speaking to parents of children and caretakers of parents: *You are obviously successful at caring for your parents despite the challenges. What is your secret sauce?*

SOCIAL/GENERAL ICEBREAKERS

1. What do you think of the movie/restaurant/5K run? Why?

2. Tell me about the best vacation you've ever taken.

3. What's your favorite thing to do on a rainy day?

4. If you could replay any moment in your life, what would it be?

5. What one thing would you really like to own? Why?

6. Tell me about one of your favorite relatives.

7. What was it like in the town where you grew up?

8. What would you like to come back as in your next life?

9. Tell me about your kids.

10. What do you think is the perfect age? Why?

11. What is a typical day like for you?

12. Of all the places you've lived, tell me about the one you like the best.

13. What's your favorite holiday? What do you enjoy about it?

14. What are some of your family traditions that you particularly enjoy?

15. Tell me about the first car you ever bought.

16. How has the Internet or social media affected your life?

17. Who were your idols as a kid? Have they changed?

18. Describe a memorable teacher you had.

19. Tell me about a movie/book you've seen or read more than once.

20. How are you holding up?

21. Tell me why you were named _____. What is the origin of your last name?

22. Tell me about a place you've visited that you hope never to return to.

23. What's the best surprise you've ever received?

24. What's the neatest surprise you've ever pulled off for someone else?

25. Skiing here is always challenging. What are some of your favorite places to ski?

26. Who would star as you in a movie about your life? Why that person?

27. Who is the most famous person you've met?

28. Tell me about some of your New Year's resolutions.

29. What's the most antiestablishment thing you've ever done?

30. Describe a costume that you wore to a party.

31. Tell me about a political position you'd like to hold.

32. What song reminds you of an incident in your life?

33. What's the most memorable meal you've eaten?

34. What's the most unforgettable coincidence you've experienced or heard about?

35. How are you able to tell if that melon is ripe?

36. What motion picture star would you like to interview? Why?

37. Tell me about your family.

38. What aroma brings forth a special memory?

39. Describe the scariest person you ever met.

40. What's your favorite thing to do when you have alone time?

41. Tell me about a childhood friend who used to get you in trouble.

42. Describe your first away-from-home living quarters or experience.

43. Tell me about a time that you lost a job.

44. Share a memory of one of your grandparents.

45. Describe an embarrassing moment you've had.

46. Tell me something most people would never guess about you.

47. What would you do if you won a million dollars?

48. Describe your ideal weather and why.

49. How did you learn to ski/hang drywall/play piano?

50. What is the number one item you would take to a deserted island?

One of my all-time favorite ways to launch a conversation in a business or social setting and get to know someone is to ask one of the many iterations of *What keeps you busy?* It is an excellent query that does not pigeonhole others based on what they do for a living, if they are married, or if they have children. No labels; instead, sincere interest in how she spends her time, allowing for numerous directions in conversation. Your conversation partner discloses whatever she chooses. This is situational as you will learn in the following examples. Count on deeper and more interesting conversation as a result.

A wonderful way to get to know someone at a professional setting is to ask: *What keeps you busy outside of work?* You will learn that your customer, colleague, stakeholder, or manager may have an array of responses. Some are busy with kids, some with graduate school, others with yoga, basement refinishing, or cooking classes. The responses are infinite, including recreational, community oriented, religious, intellectual, family, and social activities.

- When I meet someone at a volunteer event, I ask "What keeps you busy outside of volunteering?" The reply might be: "I stay at home with my kids" or "I try to get to the gym" or "I'm a mortgage broker," but in any case the conversation is off and rolling without any intrusive questions.

- At a wedding: "What keeps you busy outside of wedding celebrations?

- At back-to-school night: "What keeps you busy outside of your kids?"

- At spin class: "What keeps you busy outside of working out?"

- At church or synagogue: "What keeps you busy outside of attending services?"

- On a subway or bus: "What keeps you busy outside of commuting?"

- At your spouse's office party: "What keeps you busy outside of attending your partner's work parties?

- Talking with your high school–aged nephew or fellow student: "What keeps you busy outside of school?"

- At a Rotary meeting: "What keeps you busy outside of Rotary?"

- Waiting in line at the DMV: "What keeps you busy outside of waiting in this infuriating line?"

- On a gondola or chairlift: "What keeps you busy outside of snowboarding?"

Okay, I know you get the idea. There are occasions when I simply ask: *What keeps you busy?*, which has launched a thousand ships . . . or at least many a great conversation.

A variation of this that I will routinely use in professional settings is: *What do you do for fun?* Especially when I know we will get to the business at hand, but because it is my role to assume the burden, build rapport, and get to know the other person in a genuine way. When walking down a long hall, waiting for a delayed colleague to join a Zoom meeting, or enjoying a meal with someone that works for me, I've found that you can't lose with *What do you do for fun?* or *What keeps you busy outside of work?*

3

TAKE THE PLUNGE: START A CONVERSATION!

You are armed with a pocketful of icebreakers. You know that if someone greets you, you've got some great material for a conversation. Just having topics in mind to talk about goes a long way toward improving your skills. However, there are still a few gaps that can give you needless heart palpitations. Right now you only feel prepared to respond when someone else engages you in conversation. So you walk into your son's school and wait for another parent to say hello. You go to an industry dinner and try to act busy while you hope for a colleague to come along and talk. No. No. No. It does not need to be so stressful.

Matt McGraw, an information services manager in Denver, described how a situation was made less stressful because of his initiation of small talk. "When I was much younger, nineteen or twenty, attending the University of Oregon, I worked part-time for a couple of years at the local hospital. My job title was prep tech, and my role was to prepare the male surgical patients for surgery, which included shaving them. As you can imagine, this was a difficult job for me as well as the patient. I began my workday at four thirty a.m., so it was usually very early when I was prepping my first patient. I would spend as much as an hour or more with each one. The shaving itself was difficult and physically uncomfortable. The patients were hungry, oftentimes in pain, and weirded out by having another man shave them. Many were very sick, facing mortal fears. An open-heart prep required shaving a person one hundred percent from chin to ankles. Hopefully, I've painted the situation as difficult.

"But I soon discovered that everything would go a thousand times better if I engaged them in small talk. I found that they relaxed, and that the time went by much faster if I could draw them out of the moment. We didn't talk about their health or their fears or politics or sports, but just general, easy stuff, like where they lived, what it was like there, where they were from originally, things like that.

"I totally agree with you about the power of small talk.

It is not about an agenda but is simply a way to acknowledge a person as being very real and there. In the end, I suspect my patients talked to me more than they had a chance to talk to all of their doctors and nurses put together. It was an interesting job."

You can start the conversation—yes, *you!* It's not nearly as hard as you think. And the best part is that it puts you in charge of your own destiny. Instead of waiting for someone—anyone—to talk to you, you choose your conversation partner. What a concept: You get to select someone. You might even enjoy it!

The rules are simple. When someone gives you a smile, you are naturally inclined to smile back. Be the first to smile and greet another person. That's pretty easy. Just a smile and a few words, and it's done. Be sure that you make eye contact. That simple act is the beginning of establishing rapport. In those few seconds you have shown an interest in the other person. However, if the thought of this makes you want to jump into bed and pull the covers over your head, practice flashing your pearly whites in a setting that requires nothing more. Walk through a store and just smile and say hello to a few people as you pass them. As you cut through the parking lot into the grocery store, greet other shoppers. Keep practicing until it feels natural.

My friend Barb took a leap out of her professional comfort zone to run for city council. She's a natural at small talk anyway, but she discovered something very important during her campaign. At public forums, the other candidates would enter the room, find their place on the dais, and sit down to review their notes or prepare answers to anticipated questions. But Barb would mingle with the people in the audience, making a personal connection with as many as possible. She discovered that the best way to get people comfortable enough to open up and express themselves was to look them in the eye and ask *What's* your *name?* Making eye contact and placing the emphasis on the word *your*, rather than the word *name*, signaled to the person that they were important. She never failed to make a connection when she used this approach.

The prospect of approaching new people to start a conversation can be daunting. It takes extreme confidence for so many of us to simply start a conversation. Those that are outwardly gregarious seem to come to this talent naturally. The overwhelming fear of rejection faces most of us when we enter a reception, virtual meeting, conference room, hospitality room, or baby shower with no familiar faces in sight. I have the magic solution to erase all these fears and also to ensure we make the most of opportunities to mix and mingle.

Here it is . . . drumroll please . . . turn each of these opportunities into a task. We are by nature great at accomplishing tasks. We wear clean clothes, water our plants, create PowerPoint presentations, manage projects, and feed and shuttle children. All tasks. Not necessarily ones we love, but the tasks get done. From this moment on, turn opportunities to mix and mingle into tasks.

When entering the coffee break at a conference, awards ceremony, daughter's lacrosse banquet, Zoom meeting, or wedding reception, I have already decided how many new people I will approach. Sometimes I give myself the task of just one new person, especially in a virtual setting. If attending a networking event, then my task is probably to meet three new people. At a wedding shower where I only know the mother of the bride, then the task is likely two to four strangers. When I am making my way through the reception at an association event, the task is at least two new people, and if it is a hospitality suite or client reception, then four to five strangers approached is my task. Sure, it is not necessarily easy, especially without practice, yet turning it into a task is more easily digestible. And guess what?? When I complete my task, I gift myself with outstanding rewards!!

I allow myself a cocktail, yay! Or I go sit in the lobby

area with my device and recharge until I need to join fellow tablemates for dinner. Sometimes my reward, if appropriate . . . drumroll again . . . is departing early! How great is that? I made the most of the meeting, conference, or party, then I get home earlier than expected to enjoy alone time, finish work tasks, or hit the sack. Turning these opportunities into tasks is a great way for motivated but shy or introverted people to get the job done. And for those of you extroverted readers . . . this will require you to meet new people as well! So often extroverted people attract people without lifting a finger, rarely considering those off in the corner with no one to talk with. This is a missed opportunity to enjoy the power of meeting new people.

WHAT'S IN A NAME?

Okay, now you actually do have to stay and talk, not just offer a passing hello. Make it a point to remember the other person's name; learning and using names is probably the single most important rule of good conversation, so stay focused during the introduction. Repeat the name back in your greeting. *Nice to meet you, Debra*. To help yourself commit the name to memory, immediately use the person's name in the conversation. Most of us are thinking about the business at hand or what we are going to say next. Refrain from thinking about your reply and concentrate on the other person's name. Focus on the name, repeat it, and then formulate your answer.

If you do get distracted during the introduction and miss the name, confess! Don't go through the whole conversation pretending you know the person's name. It's better to say something like *Excuse me, I'm not sure I got your name.* It is always preferable to have the other party repeat it than to fake it. Never, ever fake it! This is especially true if, for example, you run into someone you've met previously whose name you cannot recall as you are standing in line at the movie theater or conversing with a client at an open house. Don't wait for divine inspiration. Say *I'm so sorry. I've forgotten your name. Please remind me.* This proactive tactic will prevent impending disaster. For instance, you have forgotten your client's name and in the midst of conversation your boss advances your way. How will you introduce your boss to your client if you don't know your client's name? Never put off requesting a name reminder before moving on to chatting, or you will regret it. The worst is the gambler who approaches with a sure bet: *I'll bet you don't remember my name!* As I am not inclined to up the ante, I fold immediately and ask to be reminded!

You no longer have to worry about avoiding people because you've forgotten their names. Assume the burden, tell the truth, and chances are you'll go on to have a very pleasant conversation. Even if you're on the other side of a crowded room or passing in the grocery store, go over and greet the person. If you avoid someone because you are embarrassed over having forgotten her name, you've just compounded the error with rudeness. Or equally crummy, you will be perceived as arrogant, too good to swing by to say "Hi."

Individuals with foreign or unusual names get slighted more than the rest of us. Make it a point to learn the proper pronunciation, even if it means that the other person repeats it a few times. When you take the time to learn another person's name, you are expressing a sincere interest in that individual that will be warmly received. Conversely, if you get lazy because a person has a difficult name, you are sending a message that it's not worth your trouble to learn his name. This is just as critical during video chats. Nothing easier than reading each person's name right there on the screen; there is literally no excuse to not make use of each person's name as you go back and forth. If there is a name that is not spelled out, or a name that you are unsure of the proper pronunciation, just ask!

Remembering names is well worth the effort. In fact, learning names is part of hosting the conversation. A host is always expected to know and use every person's name, since the host is responsible for making introductions as new individuals enter the conversation. An example of behaving as a host despite not being the actual host: I was seated at a table for eight and met three people who had arrived at the table before I did. As others arrived, I extended my hand, introduced myself, and made the introductions to the other three. I said, *This is Linda with Oracle, and Jon with SONY, and Sam from the Association of Safety Engineers.* Acting as the host puts everyone at ease and creates an atmosphere of warmth and appreciation that naturally encourages conversation. It also positions you as a leader in the group. Continue to behave as if you are the host whenever someone new arrives to your group.

NIX THE NICKNAMES

If a colleague introduces himself as "Michael," don't call him "Mike." If he wanted you to call him "Mike," he would have introduced himself that way. If someone has a difficult name, make the effort to learn it—do not shorten it to a nickname without permission! It makes me crazy when someone shortens my name to "Debbie."

I know I'm not alone in this. After a meeting, a woman named Julia walked up to me and said, "Debra, I've wanted to tell you something. My name used to be Debra, also. I used to give presentations for the government. Invariably, someone would call me Debbie while asking a question. I hate the name Debbie. Finally, I just couldn't stand it anymore. I changed my name to Julia!"

Make sure you use people's names and get them right! For instance, I call a client whose administrative assistant answers, *Katherine Winter's office, this is Susan.* I respond by saying, *Hi Susan. This is Debra Fine. May I speak with Katherine?* Notice that I used each person's name and did not take liberties with any of them. Susan is very important because she represents the gateway to my client. It would not serve me well to annoy her by slashing her name to "Sue," nor would it be helpful to avoid using her name altogether. Using people's names shows that you are interested in them and makes them feel special.

Another example: When I was at the ski rental returning a couple of overdue sets of skis, poles, and boots, I started talking to the clerk while we waited for my account details to show up on the computer. In the course of our brief conversation I used his name and asked if he was a skier or snowboarder. By the time my late fees showed up on-screen, he canceled them and told me to have a nice day! When you use another person's name sincerely in a conversation, it makes that person feel special.

IT'S BETTER TO GIVE THAN TO RECEIVE

It's just as important to give your name when you meet someone—even if you've met him or her previously and think they should remember your name. Consider it a random act of kindness. Extend your hand. *Hi, Patrick, Debra Fine. How are you?* By stating my name, I let Patrick off the hook. If he had forgotten my name, it didn't show, and he didn't have to waste conversation time being distracted trying to recall my name.

My current, second, and very last husband is a periodontist. As a group, periodontists are not known for their charm or gregarious personalities. Frequently, when we go out, his patients recognize him and start a conversation without reintroducing themselves. My husband doesn't have a clue who they are and feels awkward. He can't include me in the conversation easily because he can't get through the introductions. Sure, I wish he would ask to be reminded, and of course I extend my hand giving the gift of my name and asking for theirs, assuming the burden for my husband. Don't ever assume that someone who sees you infrequently will remember your name, especially when they see you out of context. You will remember the Realtor who spent a Sunday driving you around looking at houses easier than she will remember you, especially if you are in sweats at the gas station. Cut her some slack; offer your name when you say hello.

One last tip on names. When you find yourself in a setting with throngs of people whom you may or may not know, such as an annual neighborhood BBQ or a friend's milestone birthday, instead of saying *Nice to meet you* try *It's nice to see you*. Some folks are put off if they have met you before yet you say "Nice to meet you." "But we have met before!" she exclaims. As time goes on, our database of names and faces becomes too much to remember, so a good out is *Good to see you*.

4

KEEP THE CONVERSATION GOING!

Remember, instead of sitting back and waiting for another kind soul to start a conversation, take the lead. Think of it as if you invited that person to your home for dinner. As host, it's your job to see that your guest is comfortable. The same is true in conversation—try to make your guest as comfortable as possible. When you walk into a party or a gathering, find a person to meet. It's much easier to engage one person rather than enter a group conversation, so begin by looking for the "approachable person."

The approachable person is the one who makes eye contact with you or who is not actively engaged in a conversation or another activity, such as scrolling on her device or working at his desk. It's the solitary person getting a bite to eat in the buffet line, someone sitting alone at a table, or the one standing to the side after services. More often than not, these people are relieved to have someone else initiate the conversation. Believe me, I've been around plenty of these folks—they are intelligent, interesting, welcoming . . . and shy. They are in the same spot you were before you decided to improve your skills. If you take the conversational plunge, they will herald you as a savior.

Make it a point to look around a room when you first enter it. It doesn't matter what the event is—a meeting, a reception, a baby shower, a party, even a family reunion—there are people standing alone or sitting at an empty table. Don't wait; make eye contact and be the first to smile. You'll net a smile back, and you'll put the other person at ease, the way any fine host would! People will reward you by being attentive listeners and giving you a chance to practice your icebreakers. Don't forget: If you feel overwhelmed, simply turn it into a task.

Not only are icebreakers a good way to start a conversation, but some of the statements are accompanied by questions you can ask to keep the ball rolling. Don't use a statement alone. Using a statement by itself is like lobbing the conversational ball blindfolded, not knowing where it will land or whether it will get tossed back. For example, enthusiastic exclamations like *What a beautiful day*, or *That was a great show*, or *Long meeting* are indirect invitations to chat. Better to be direct, so there is no doubt you are starting a dialogue. Try these:

Starting with a Statement

- What a beautiful day. What's your favorite season of the year?
- I was truly touched by that movie. How did you like it? Why?
- Gas prices are high. When was the last time you had to fill your tank?
- This is a wonderful restaurant. What is your favorite restaurant? Why?
- What a great conference! Tell me about the sessions you attended.
- I was absent last week. What did I miss?
- Commuting to work has become a huge stressor. What's it like for you?
- That was an interesting program after lunch. What did you think?

- Presidential campaigns seem to start immediately after the inauguration. What do you think of the campaign process?
- I am so frustrated with getting this business off the ground. Do you have any ideas?

Starting with a Statement

- I am excited about our new mayor. How do you think her administration will be different from her predecessor's?
- Working from home sure has its advantages. How has it worked for you?
- Your lawn always looks so green. What is your secret?
- We've been working together for months now. I'd like to get to know you better. Tell me about some of your outside interests.
- You worked pretty hard on that stair stepper. What other equipment do you use?
- You always wear such attractive clothes. What are your favorite stores?
- What a beautiful home. How do you manage to run a house with four children?
- I listen to a lot of podcasts, how about you?

EASY OPENERS

Like most things that are unfamiliar, starting a conversation appears harder than it actually is. If you still feel uncertain, listen to this true story. A national news show put a hidden microphone on a gentleman and set him loose at a party. His mission was to start as many conversations with women as possible using the ridiculous icebreaker *Hi. What's your sign?* Here we are in a new millennium, and he was using that infamous 1970s line! And it worked! He walked up to a woman, smiled, and spoke his line. She responded by saying, *Taurus. What's yours?*

He answered with, *Libra. Do you know much about astrology?* They went on to have a very interesting conversation. The moral of the story is that it's the effort that counts. What matters is taking the plunge and starting the conversation. This gentleman was successful because he showed an interest in what the other person had to say, and she was open to it. Of course showing genuine interest is flattering and essential to conversing. If you are interested in how I lost sixty-five pounds or how I started my business or anything else about me, I feel special. I also think positively about you and want to continue talking with you. The more interest you show in me, the more interesting you become to me. The simple act of truly being interested in the other person has an amazing effect on the conversation—it just snowballs!

You will be successful if you just take the initiative and give it a try. You'll be surprised by how easy it is and at the positive reinforcement you get from people when you start a conversation. Remember the following four steps and you are well on your way to an excellent chat.

1. Make eye contact.
2. Smile.
3. Find that approachable person!
4. Offer your name and use theirs.

Give it a try. You'll discover that it's really worthwhile. The true effort is taking the risk to be the first to say hello. There is no perfect icebreaker. *What's your sign?* is a huge risk as an icebreaker. As silly as it was, it worked because the woman decided she would allow the man to engage her in conversation. Think about it. We all do that. We size someone up, determine if we are in the mood to chat, and gauge whether it is worth our investment of time. The persons being approached have already decided on their willingness to respond, regardless of the words said.

Often, people make the huge mistake of assuming they will have nothing in common with another person. We easily allow differences of all kinds to bias us against engaging in conversation. We allow gender, ethnicity, social status, generation, occupation, lifestyle, and a host of other differences to create artificial barriers to success. In the course of touring the country and talking to thousands of people in every geographic region, from all walks of life, I have affirmed that we are all more alike than we are different. It's simply a matter of talking, showing an interest, and listening. When I approach a conversation, I'm slowly peeling an onion—just one layer at a time. I am always amazed and gratified by how interesting and worthwhile it is to take the time to talk with a stranger.

At one of the first programs I presented, I asked everyone to introduce himself or herself and tell why they came to a session on small talk. The first person to introduce himself was a gentleman named Bob. He said he was attending because he was a Motorola customer-service engineer, and his boss wanted him to improve his conversational skills with customers. He added that, although his boss sent him to the session, he was glad because he'd just moved to the very small town of Elizabeth, Colorado. As a single man alone, he felt isolated and wanted to meet people. Here's what followed:

Debra: Elizabeth, Colorado, Bob. I used to live in Elizabeth. I lived next to the Douglas County line near the town of Parker. Are you there or closer to the town of Elizabeth itself?

Bob: No, I live near Parker as well in a development called Ponderosa Park Estates.

Debra: Ponderosa Park Estates? Wow. Bob, I used to live there, too! I lived right near Ponderosa Lane and Overlook Road.

Bob: Well, Debra, I live on Overlook Road.

Debra: That is amazing, Bob. I lived in the log house at 120 Overlook Road.

Bob: Well, Debra, this is truly amazing because I live in the log house at 120 Overlook Road!

It turns out that when the family to whom my ex-husband and I sold the home in 1985 moved, they sold it to Bob. Because of this chance encounter, and because I took an interest in the fact that Bob was from Elizabeth, Bob invited me to bring my family to see the house again.

I was delighted. We visited Bob at his house, and my kids got the chance to experience a part of their own history that would otherwise have been lost to them since they were too young to remember having lived there.

Make the effort, and you'll be richly rewarded. You have a jumbo-sized list of icebreakers to get you started, and *What's your sign?* isn't even on it!

BREAKING IN IS HARD TO DO

You've finally gotten up enough nerve to go speak to that one person you're most determined to meet. But he's busy chatting away with someone else. How do you break in? While the polite thing to do would be to wait until you get noticed, sometimes the conversation can be so engrossing that you will never be granted an audience unless you take the initiative. In the meantime, you feel a little foolish just standing alone in the presence of these two people who are fully occupied with each other.

The best approach I've found for breaking in is a throwback to bygone dances. In a gentler era, when a man wanted to dance with a woman but she already had a dance partner, all the man had to do was politely tap her dance partner on the shoulder, and the partner would relinquish his turn with the woman.

When you approach a "dancing couple," wait politely for an interval and then turn to the person you have no desire to speak with and ask for permission to intrude so that you may speak with his or her conversation partner. Most people are too gracious to say no and will give you their permission. You've smoothly maneuvered yourself into a position of attention with the audience of your choice, and you've done it skillfully and politely. Another option that is less intrusive is to excuse yourself for the interruption, noting that you wanted to let the person know you were in attendance and wanted an opportunity to get together before the evening was over. You will either be included at that point or instead searched out at a later time. Either way, the person knows you made the effort to touch base.

PARTY OF FIVE

It's tough for a conversational novice to break into a two-person chat, let alone a group of five or more. A group this size is usually well entrenched, and it requires covert operations to infiltrate. Use these tactics when you find it necessary or desirable to get engaged with these folks:

- **Show interest in the speaker, but stand slightly away from the group.** A group this size is slow to warm, so first let them become accustomed to seeing you. Slowly, they will shift to bring you into the circle.

- **Ease into the group by demonstrating that you've been listening.** Look for welcoming signs such as them asking your opinion or physically shifting positions to better include you.

- **Initially, it is best to find a point of agreement; barring that, just acknowledge the speaker.** Wait before rocking the boat with a big wave of radical opinions. Before offering your views, let the group warm to you. If you come on too strong too fast, the group will resent your intrusion and disband. Then you have to start all over again, looking to chat with someone you haven't just offended!

- **Lastly, if there is a familiar face in the group, quietly extend your hand, letting her know you wish to say hello when she has a moment later in the evening.** Your hope is to be invited into the group. If not, nothing lost but lots gained. She knows you acknowledged her and even if you do not connect later, you have made a positive impression by simply saying hello.

5

LET'S GIVE 'EM SOMETHING TO
TALK ABOUT

You've smiled, made eye contact, found the approachable person, offered your name, and used theirs. What's left, you ask? Plenty! Have no fear—this is where it really gets fun. If you are introverted, you will love this part because you stay on the quiet side. Your mission is to get your conversation partners talking about themselves. Most people enjoy the opportunity to share their stories, and if you give them the chance, they'll start talking. This is a no-brainer route to small-talking success.

IT'S ALL IN THE ASKING

By asking open-ended questions, you offer your conversation partner the opportunity to disclose as much or as little as she wants. These questions demand more than a simple yes or no answer, yet they make no stressful demands. Your partner will decide how much she feels comfortable saying. Such questions are effective with coworkers, kids, neighbors, in-laws, industry colleagues, friends, and when first making the acquaintance of a stranger. The key to successfully using open-ended questions is choosing the right question and then following up with another if it's needed.

OPEN-ENDED QUESTIONS

- Describe for me . . .

- Tell me about . . .

- How did you . . . ?

- What was that like for you?

- What brought you to . . . ?

- Why?

For instance, let's take the toughest conversation partners of all: school-age kids. They make it so difficult to have a conversation, it's almost an oxymoron to consider them conversation partners. Nonetheless, because they are kids, I give them the benefit of the doubt and hone my skills with my own two kids. I know I haven't lost my edge when I get them engaged in a meaningful dialogue.

My kids come through the door at the end of the day, and I ask, *How was your day at school?* In stereo, I get back, *Fine.* Instead of considering that a dead end, I follow up with another question. I inquire, *What did you like about it today?* My teenage son usually says, *I don't know.* I look him right in the eye and tell him, *Really, tell me about one class you liked today.* He thinks about it for a minute. Finally he says, *Science.* And I inquire, *What did you like about science?* He launches into a colorful description of an experiment they did, and we're talking. The bottom line is that you have to open it up, and you have to show you truly care.

Some Great Kid Conversation Starters:

- Do you like being a big sister?
- What makes you mad? What makes you happy?
- Do you have a pet? Do you wish you had a pet?

- Do you enjoy sports? Why?
- What is your favorite food and why?
- Why did you decide to draw a unicorn?
- During your free time, what is your favorite activity?

Here are a few tips on ways to form connected relationships with younger people instead of relationships dependent on inanimate objects such as social media or text:

- When you are with your children, be WITH them. Don't just put down your smartphone, put it away. Once it is out of sight, it's less likely to distract you and shows your child that he is the priority.

- Say out loud to your child, "I am going to do some work (schedule a dentist appointment, call a friend, etc.) in a bit on my cell phone, but right now I really want to spend some time with you. Tell me about your day."

- Create boundaries around technology and apply the rules to everyone, including you and the other members of the household. If you've agreed to a no-phones-at-the-table rule or devices off by 9 p.m., it should apply to everyone, not just your children.

- Teach your children the art of conversation by practicing with them. Ask open-ended questions of them and answer their questions thoughtfully and thoroughly. Skip the one-word answers or the distracted "uh-huh" when you are with them.

- When you do, in fact, call them on their phone, set the expectation that they should answer or call you back. Too often phone calls receive a text in return. Why? Text is easier, safer, and less taxing than a phone conversation. But if your child is taking the easy way out of making a connection with you, imagine how difficult it will be for them to have a conversation with a teacher, coach, or new friend.

DIGGING DEEPER

Every Monday in offices across the country people ask each other, *How was your weekend?* That question most often nets a one-sentence reply akin to, *Good. How about yours?* Before a reply is even uttered, you are ten steps down the hall. What's the message? That you really weren't interested, you were just saying hello. *How was your vacation? How was your holiday? How's work? How are you? What's been going on? How have you been?* These everyday inquiries are just a few other ways of saying hello. It's almost universally understood that these questions are a form of greeting, not a sincere inquiry. Only in North America are there these rhetorical questions. In most other cultures and countries *How are you?* really means *How are you?* It would be considered rude to ask that question and not expect an answer.

Most of the time the conversation ends immediately after a brief exchange. I ask my husband, Steve, *How was your day?* He replies, *Great.* The conversation evaporates—not because there was no place to go with it but because of a lack of follow-up. My husband doesn't think I really care about his day unless I ask more. I invite conversation by saying, *What made it so great? What went on for you today?*

The following script illustrates a conversation mired in a rut of clichés:

Debra: Hi, Jon! How are you today?

Jon: I'm feeling pretty blue.

Debra: Well, Jon, keep your chin up!

Jon: I think I might get laid off!

Debra: Good jobs are few and far between.

Jon: Do you think I should start looking for a new job right away?

Debra: If you don't lift a finger you could be out in the cold, perhaps not even able to bring home the bacon much less keep body and soul together, and wouldn't that be a fine kettle of fish?

Jon: What do you think the best approach would be? Looking through the online posts or LinkedIn job posts?

Debra: Sure. Take the bull by the horns. Put your best foot forward and face the music. You are no babe in the woods and you're not getting any younger. If you go at it you might get more offers than you can shake a stick at!

Whenever you begin a dialogue with a question, get ready to dig deeper so that the other person knows you are interested in hearing more. Digging in deeper indicates you truly desire a response and are prepared to invest time in hearing the response. Here are some suggestions:

- How was your summer? *Excellent*. What special things did you do?
- How were your holidays? *Pretty good*. How did you celebrate?
- How was your weekend? *Good*. What did you do? *I went to see that new play down at the Civic Center*. Really? You're interested in _____? I never knew that. Tell me more about that.
  - Did you do anything relaxing?
  - Is that something you usually do on the weekend?
- How's the project? *Good*. What have you been working on most recently?

With the right queries, a conversation with a coworker about the weekend can occupy an entire cup of coffee. The key is to have a genuine interest in what the other person is saying, along with a genuine desire to hear the response. So while you get to be quiet, you do not get to be passive. You must actively participate in the conversation.

Suppose, however, you call a customer or your boss, and the conversation is as follows when you ask about the weekend:

> *How was your weekend?* Great. *Tell me about it.*
>
> Well, we spent some time working in the garden and that was about it. Now about this proposal.

You should recognize that the other person has steered the conversation back to business. That's the signal that the person does not want to chat at the moment. Respect those wishes by switching into a business mode.

Here are some other examples of digging deeper into a conversation: You ask, *How have you been?* and get the reply, *Busy.* Follow-up responses could include: *How do you deal with being busy? What is going on that's got you so busy? Describe a busy day for you. Do you like being busy? Does there seem to be a cycle of busy-ness during your year? Do you remember a time in your life when you weren't as busy?*

Or you ask, *Isn't this weather terrible?* and receive the reply, *It sure is.* You might respond with these: *How terrible does it get in this part of the country? What is your idea of an ideal climate? How does bad weather affect you? Have you lived anywhere else with terrible weather? What brought you here? What is the worst weather you have endured?*

I received this note from a director-level executive at a large aerospace corporation demonstrating the benefits of "digging deeper." He relates how he emailed a colleague about her recent job promotion. *How's the new job?* Her reply: *Pretty good.* Instead of accepting that brief reply, he emailed her back: *I'm really interested . . . how has it been for you?* This got him a detailed email response about the pitfalls and challenges of her new position.

Of course it's much easier to ask appropriate open-ended questions of people you know than those you are just meeting. Use discretion when meeting new people: Asking a difficult question could put the other person in an awkward position. Likewise, sometimes when we are asking open-ended questions, we really are asking questions that require only a one- or two-word answer. Here are some new ways to ask old favorites:

Instead of asking:	Try this:
Are you married?	**Tell me about your family.**
What do you do for a living?	**Tell me about your business/work.**

Do you have kids?	**Tell me about your family.**
What's your favorite hobby?	**Tell me about your favorite hobby.**
How was your weekend?	**What was the best part of your weekend? What went on for you this weekend?**

When you need to mingle at an industry function or take a client to lunch, prepare yourself for the event by selecting some business-related questions to ask. See pages 23–24 for some that work every time. Of course, the goal is not to ask every one of these but to have some ready so that you feel prepared, poised, and confident.

FREE FOR THE TAKING

If you are an astute observer, you'll discover that your small-talking cohort is giving you a wealth of free information you can use to keep a conversation going. Sources of free information include:

Answers to open-ended questions. When you invite someone to tell you about his family or her job, you will receive additional free information that you can use to further the conversation. Suppose you ask me, *Debra, how is it that you worked in product planning for AT&T?* and I say, *I was in R&D in Buffalo, New York, where I'm from, and I hated it. I hated being an engineer—they don't even make pocket protectors for women! So I asked to be transferred anywhere. They brought me to Denver to work in product planning.* I offered lots of free information: I'm from Buffalo, I was in R&D (research and development), and I hated being an engineer. You can choose any of that free information to find out more about what interests you the most. You could facilitate the conversation by asking any one of a dozen questions, including:

- *Are the winters in Buffalo really as bad as they say?*

- *Why didn't you like being an engineer?*

- *Would it have made a difference in your career if there had been pocket protectors for women?*

- *What is it like to do R&D for a corporation like AT&T?*

- *Was it tough living in a city with a perennial Super Bowl loser?*

- *Where did you study engineering?*

Stay focused on responses for any details or free information that you can use to keep the conversation going.

Appearances. Lapel pins and jewelry: The man behind me in line at the bakery was wearing a lapel pin on his suit. I asked him about it and found out that he's in the local Rotary Club. From that inauspicious beginning we had a great conversation. I shared with him that I was a Rotarian as well.

Team apparel and other logo-identified clothing, accessories, water bottles, and clipboards are great conversation starters. Be observant for a new hairdo, a book or magazine, a child's artwork, or a cast on a broken limb. If his phone is out, ask about his favorite app, or why he prefers Apple over Android. Some options:

- *It looks like you might be a fan of the Denver Broncos. What do you think of their season?*

- *I notice that you're wearing a shirt from the London Hard Rock Café. Have you been there? What did you think of it?*

- *I see that you ran the Race for the Cure; what other races have you run?*

Fail-Safe Questions for Every Business Function

- How did you get started in your business?
- How did you come up with this idea?
- What got you interested in _____ (business function, job, industry)?
- What happened first?
- Tell me what you enjoy most about your profession.
- What separates your firm from the competition?
- Describe some of the challenges of your profession.
- What will be the coming trends in your business?
- What ways have you found to be the most effective in promoting your business?
- Tell me about your most important work experience.
- What advice would you give someone just starting out in your business?
- What one thing would you do if you knew for sure that you couldn't fail?
- What significant changes have you seen since you started in your field?
- What is the most bizarre incident that you've ever experienced in your business?
- What is the biggest plus for you working from home? Greatest negative?

- What do you dislike about video chat?
- How has technology improved your work life?
- How has the Internet impacted your business? What about your profession as a whole?
- How has Covid (or any global event) impacted your work?
- Tell me how you incorporate social media into your work or personal life.

Office and home decor are small-talk opportunities waiting to happen.

- A diploma on the wall gives you an opening: *What made you choose the University of Michigan for your graduate work?*

- Virtually any object or photograph on display is a conversation starter: *You must love golf—tell me about this trophy.*

- *What an interesting piece of art. Tell me about it.*

- *Tell me about this picture. Who is that with you?*

Location, location, location and occasion, occasion,

occasion. The location and occasion of an event offer a wide variety of free information. At a wedding: *I was the bride's college roommate. How do you know the couple?* At a seminar or convention, simply asking *What brought you to this event?* is an easy and unobtrusive way to start a conversation. An easy and reliable piece of free information is to simply ask, *Did you grow up here?* If she did grow up "here," learn where else she would live if she could. If he grew up somewhere else, find out what brought him to where you live now. On the subway, airplane, or bus, ask your seatmate: *Going home or leaving home?*

As I took leave of a seminar I had taught, I held the elevator for a man coming down the hall. I usually don't small talk on elevators because of the limited time, but on a whim I used the free information I had, which was that I knew there were two classrooms on that floor. Since the man had not been in my class, it was a pretty good guess that he'd come from the other. I asked him, *Were you here for a class?* He told me he'd attended a book-writing class. It turns out that I was speaking with Harry MacLean, best-selling author and teacher of the course. We continued our conversation outside of the elevator, and I now have a new friend. He even agreed to speak to my book club about his then most recent book, *Once Upon a Time.* One of the reasons I love small talk is that you just never know who you'll meet or where it'll lead.

Behavior. If you are observant, you'll get a lot of free information from people's behavior. The way they speak and write can offer you small-talk starters. Notice if they are left-handed. You can inquire, *Is it challenging being left-handed? What pet peeves do you have about it?* Does the person have an accent? If so, you might say, *I thought I heard an accent. What part of the country/world are you from?* or *What brought you here?* or *What do you miss the most about where you are from?* or *What do you enjoy about your new home?*

I entered my local FedEx office with efficiency in mind—after all, that's why I'm there. I want to get in and get out. The very fact that I require the services of FedEx is free information that I'm in a hurry. I've got a pressing delivery. However, as I watched the clerk complete the forms, I was struck by the beautiful handwriting of this left-handed woman. I complimented her with a statement—not a question. Unfortunately, she responded as though it were an inquiry. I got the whole story of how she used to be a teacher and had purposefully perfected her handwriting . . . she moved to Arizona . . . got divorced . . . remarried and moved to Colorado. I could not get her to understand that I was in a hurry. She was still talking as I backed out of the door! That is what I call an unintended icebreaker. It goes to show you that the slightest interest in someone is often all it takes to get a conversation going. Even the one-sided kind!

FAKE IT TILL YOU MAKE IT

Now that you are becoming small-talk savvy, practice the fundamentals. Can you recall five surefire questions to use in a business setting? Can you name half a dozen sources of free information? Scout your current location right now. What do you see that would make good conversation material?

You'll become skilled at small talk the same way you've improved in other activities—practice. It's not difficult—high school geometry was much harder than this. All you need to do is practice. Little by little, you'll give your conversation partner plenty to talk about!

6

Hearing Aids and Listening Devices

We've covered half the requirements for carrying on a good conversation: how to take the lead, break the ice, and maintain a conversation. You know what works and what doesn't or you will learn as you continue to assume the burden and take the risk. However, none of this guarantees success just yet. A great conversation hinges on two things: the talking and the listening. Research has shown that people are capable of listening to approximately 300 words per minute. On the flip side, most of us can only speak at 150 to 200 words per minute—unless you're one of those folks rattling off the disclaimer at the end of a radio spot advertising a new car lease!

The dilemma is that we have the capacity to take in much more information than one person can divulge at any given time. So what do we do with this excess capacity? We put it to good use, of course. We eavesdrop on other conversations; we start thinking about what to have for dinner; we drift away into our private thoughts—and suddenly we've drifted too far . . . and missed something important!

Psychologist Carl Rogers once said, "The biggest block to personal conversation is one man's inability to listen intelligently, understandingly, and skillfully to another person." Psychoanalyst Dr. Ann Appelbaum understood the source of her livelihood when she wrote in the Menninger Clinic's newsletter *Perspective*, "The image of the voice crying in the wilderness epitomizes the loneliness, the madness of not being heard. So great is our need and hunger for validation that good listeners are prized. Psychoanalysts, for example, earn a living by listening and providing responses that validate the other person."

Have you ever gone out to lunch with someone who really needs to talk? You hardly say a word. You offer support, a few kind words, a nod of the head, and you listen. The other person feels much better afterward and is ever so grateful for the conversation.

In our technology-driven world the bombardment of constant stimuli and white noise makes it a challenge to listen. Listening is no longer taken for granted. In fact, it's frequently the exception. Attentive listening has three parts: visual, verbal, and mental. Combine these elements, and powerful listening results.

Listening?

LISTENING IS SEEN, NOT JUST HEARD

The physiological process of listening is invisible to the observer. We cannot watch the sound vibrations go into someone's ears to confirm that they received the intended message. Consequently, the speaker is always on the lookout for cues to validate receipt of the message. Visual cues, which offer the easiest form of feedback, let the speaker know you are paying attention. Facial expressions, head nods, and positive body language are clear ways of expressing interest in your conversation partner's words.

Eight-year-old Nicholas came home from school, bounded into the house, and started telling his dad about his great day at school. "Dad," Nick said, "I had a great day at school. We had art class today, and I painted a cool picture of the mountains. We played soccer during gym and I scored a goal. And guess what—they served pizza for lunch!" Nicholas looks at his dad scrolling on his device and sighs, "Dad, you're not listening to me!" His dad looks up and says, "Yes I am, son. You painted a picture of the mountains, you scored a goal in the soccer game, and you had pizza for lunch." Nicholas, unappeased, replies, "No, Dad. That's not it. You're not listening to me with your eyes."

Even though Nick's dad clearly heard his son, Nick felt minimized because he did not have his dad's full attention. He wanted more than a download of facts about his day to his dad. He wanted to see his dad's response. He wanted to feel connected. He wanted his dad to be invested in the story. He wanted validation while he was telling his story.

Listening is more than just hearing. It's a level of involvement that goes beyond reciting the contents of the conversation. Ray Birdwhistell, a pioneer in nonverbal communication, estimated that in a normal two-person conversation, verbal components carry less than 35 percent of the social meaning of the situation, while nonverbal components account for over 65 percent. It's critical to maintain eye contact when you are listening to another person.

This applies to virtual interactions as well. Eye contact is made when you look directly at the camera lens. It is so easy to be distracted looking at ourselves (yes I am vain) on the monitor rather than directing your eyes to the lens. A handy hack I use is to tape a picture of our dog immediately above the lens, which reminds me to keep my eyes looking up there. Multitasking pulls us away from great eye contact. Be certain this is the impression you wish to signal to others in attendance before allowing yourself to look down at another device or type away on your keyboard. It will make a great positive impression leaving your video on, rather than a blank screen with your picture, so that others are able view you, understanding that circumstances may not always allow for a live video.

When face-to-face, don't look around at what others are doing—stay focused on the conversation at hand. Add nodding to your visual listening cues. This reinforces to the speaker that you are following along. Most people with good intentions provide eye contact. But even those with good intentions drop the conversational ball when in groups of three or more. As we glance at new arrivals or peruse the buffet table, we expect that the others in our group are maintaining eye contact. After all, it was someone else at the table that posed the question or encouraged the conversation. They won't notice our momentary lack of attention. Yet it is noticed. And one of two consequences occurs. Either the person speaking fears that we are bored so he clams up, or it is assumed that we are arrogant or rude because of our lack of good manners. When talking with people, behave as if there are no distractions in the room. It is always okay to disclose that you need to keep your eyes on the door because you promised to keep an eye out for a friend's arrival. Then your lack of consistent eye contact is explained.

Body language also gives the speaker clues about you and your listening. The following illustration demonstrates negative and positive body language. When you cross your arms and legs, you are exhibiting defensiveness—even if your reason is cold weather! If you keep your head down and avoid eye contact, you send a message that you are avoiding interaction—even if your reason is shyness and you actually want someone to talk to you! People generally respond to these signals by ignoring you; you are not considered approachable. If you rest your chin in your hand, it appears that you are bored. Likewise, when you place your hands on your hips, you appear aggressive and unhappy with your conversation partner, or with the words you are hearing. Our newest crutch is our mobile devices. Take a look around a restaurant, a reception, a bridal shower. People viewing their devices, handheld and wrist, ear buds implying activity. It is unavoidable to not assume someone is either rude or unapproachable, even those who may simply be shy while trying to look busy. Don't be that person. Leave the room if need be to take an important call or respond to an email or text. Put the ear buds away at parties, receptions, services, and similar occasions. All of the above should be at the ready when you wish to be quiet and by yourself at a coffee house or on the subway.

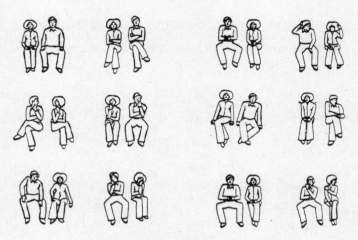

Engaging Approachable Body Language

There are just as many ways to signal your interest and enthusiasm for the dialogue.

POSITIVE MESSAGES TO THE SPEAKER

- Lean forward

- Maintain eye contact

- Open up your arms and body

- Relax your body posture

- Face your partner

- Nod and smile

OFF-PUTTING GESTURES YOU
SHOULD NEVER USE

- Pointing

- Covering your mouth

- Rubbing or fondling body parts

- Fiddling with jewelry

- Tapping a pencil or pen

- Swinging your leg

- Crossing arms across your chest

- Putting hands on your hips

- Glancing away from the person who is speaking

- Holding your device in your hand or placing it on the dining table. This suggests you are open to distraction.

Unlike other small-talking tricks that are easier than they look, these can be harder. Most of us are on automatic pilot when it comes to our body language because of a lifetime of habits. Our shoulders hunch over at a party because we are shy, we tug and twist our hair because we are nervous, we sit stiffly during a job interview because of tension. Be aware of what your body language is saying to the world. It requires practice and concentration to overcome nervous habits and use positive body language. Stick with it; practice will make it easier every time. Virtual meetings can seem like a spotlight is homing in on us. It almost feels like everyone on the call is looking at us, whereas at a face-to-face meeting we could sort of be invisible unless called on. Tackle this discomfort with the reminder that everyone is not looking at you. Unless of course you are a celebrity, wearing a clown hat, or have a fly perched on your forehead.

Here's a little trick for you. If you're uncomfortable maintaining full-on eye contact with your conversation partner, look them right between the eyes. Somehow, this little shift will make both of you feel more comfortable. It can be disconcerting to have someone staring straight into your eyes. A little polite acquiescence will make both of you feel connected but comfortable.

You can also increase the comfort level of your conversation partner by modifying your own style to be more similar to hers. If you are chatting with someone who speaks slowly and softly, work to keep your volume low as well. You can overwhelm a slow-talking, soft-spoken person with your own volume and speed. This is not to say you shouldn't be yourself; you should. However, as the "host," you want to enhance the comfort of your guest.

VERBALIZE YOUR LISTENING

Verbal cues complement the visual feedback you give a speaker. The absence of verbal cues makes a speaker wonder if anyone is listening. I called my dad, who lives in Buffalo. I was telling him a story about the kids, and there was silence on the other end of the phone. I abruptly stopped the story and asked, "Dad, are you there?" He became indignant and said, "Of course I'm here. I'm listening to you. Tell me about my grandkids." I replied, "You weren't saying anything so I thought maybe you'd suddenly been buried by eight feet of snow." "I didn't want to interrupt," he replied.

There are numerous verbal cues to let the speaker know you are fully engaged in the conversation. These brief comments tell the speaker that you are interested and want to know more. You can use verbal cues to show that you have a positive response, that you disagree, or that you want to hear more about something in particular. Check out this list to see which cues are used in different situations.

If you want to show that you are:	Say:
Interested in hearing more . . .	*Tell me more. What was that like for you?*
Taking it all in . . .	*Hmmm, I see . . .*
Responding positively . . .	*How interesting! What an accomplishment!*
Diverging . . .	*On the other hand, what do you think . . . ?*
Expanding on the idea . . .	*Along that same line, do you . . . ? Why?*
Arguing/refuting . . .	*What proof do you have of that?*
Involving yourself . . .	*Could I do that? What would it mean to me?*
Clarifying . . .	*I'm not sure I'm clear on your feelings about . . .*
Empathizing . . .	*That must have been tough/ frustrating, et cetera.*

If you want to show that you are:	Say:
Probing . . .	*What do you mean by that? How were you able to manage?*
Seeking specifics . . .	*Can you give me an example?*
Seeking generalities . . .	*What's the big picture here?*
Looking to the future . . .	*What do you think will happen next?*
Reviewing the past . . .	*What happened first?*
Seeking likenesses/ differences . . .	*Have you ever seen anything like this? What's the opposing point of view?*
Seeking extremes/ contrasts . . .	*What's the downside? What's the optimum?*

Other verbal listening cues function to redirect the conversation by transitioning to another topic. Examples of cues that offer a seamless segue include:

- That reminds me of . . .

- When you were talking about _____, I
  remembered . . .

- You know, I was just reading a post about . . .

- I've always wanted to ask you . . .

- I thought of you when I heard . . .

- Do you mind if I change the subject?

- There's something I've wanted to ask of someone
  with your expertise.

All these verbal cues indicate that you are fully present. Just as important, these cues encourage others to continue speaking. Imagine someone asks you a question, and you respond with a one-sentence answer. You are uncertain as to how much information they are truly interested in learning. Added verbal cues as you respond assure you that their interest is sincere. Verbal cues encourage others to continue. Use verbal cues as an active way to get others to do the talking so that you can spend some time eating your cheeseburger!

Interacting via text, email, and social media requires a quick response—a simple thumbs-up, haha, or heart icon indicates that you are listening and following. If nothing else, this cue acknowledges the writer. The use of these icons will many times keep the conversation going, but no matter what occurs, the messenger knows that they have been heard. On virtual platforms such as Zoom, WebEx, and Teams, thumbs-up icons along with written comments in the chat keep attendees engaged, enhancing collaboration.

A friendly reminder: don't dodge the phone feature on your phone. We rarely use it anymore ("too intrusive," "I might be interrupting an activity"). Yet the benefits of hearing a voice, the tone, the pace, the verbal cues are a huge enhancement to cultivating a connection.

Is Talking Better Than Texting? Yes. Yes, It Is.

I distinctly remember my teenage years being tethered to the phone. The actual phone, attached to a wall with a cord that, with effort, could be stretched an impressive distance.

And here we are still attached to the phone; a different phone that is tiny and cordless and knows more about us than our doctor or significant other. But here's the thing: we rarely use this little addictive contraption to actually *speak*. Sure, smartphones are good for playing games or snapping photos or ignoring a text from your mother or boss or child or whoever is on The List that day, but its intended original purpose was for speaking.

So why don't we talk anymore? Because email and texting and various forms of social media have taken over the world, which is actually making it harder, not easier, to get any real work accomplished. Plus, talking seems scarier than typing because you actually have to *talk.*

We need to remind ourselves of the benefits of face-to-face communication and the beauty and value of having *actual* conversations with *actual* humans.

Granted face-to-face communications are harder to come by, but voice-to-voice communication is right there in your pocket. Literally. So use texting and email, but use it to confirm a meeting rather than replace a meeting because believe it or not, more real business gets done when real conversations happen.

Is Talking Better Than Texting? Yes. Yes, It Is.

The *Harvard Business Review* published a piece on the success of face-to-face communication versus the success of an email or text. How much more successful are we with face-to-face communication? Thirty-four times more. As a teenager would say: That's, like, a lot.

Gabby people seldom listen. Those of us who consider ourselves quiet often congratulate ourselves for our awesome listening skills; at least we keep our mouths shut and listen! But this attitude is sometimes reflected as a lack of participation in the conversation. Too much listening and not enough verbalizing can halt a conversation, too. It is important to verbally let others know that we are following along, actively listening.

STATING THE OBVIOUS

When you paraphrase what's been said, or repeat the specifics of what you have heard, there can be no doubt that you have listened and understood the speaker. This is especially effective when you are disagreeing with your conversation partner or have listened to her explain something highly complex or technical. Paraphrasing the speaker clarifies that you understood accurately. Or it can help the speaker recognize that you misunderstood what she was attempting to communicate. For instance: I am unhappy with what I perceive as lack of help from my husband with household chores. We discuss the problem. I am thrilled when Steve promises to help more around the house. Two weeks later I jump all over him. I am upset because I have not witnessed his added help around the house. "You promised to help more with household chores. When do you plan to start keeping your promise?" I implore. "I am helping out," Steve replies. "I've been collecting the trash and taking it to the curb every Thursday." "That's it?" I ask. I expected Steve to take on 50 percent of the chores. But instead of clarifying what he meant by agreeing to my request for help, I assumed he knew what I meant. He assumed I meant any help would be appreciated. Men and women will say exactly the same words and yet mean two entirely different things. Clarify or paraphrase to prevent misunderstandings at work and at home.

In an emotionally charged situation, you gain a side benefit of defusing anger when you repeat the specifics of what the other person stated. People naturally calm down when they realize they've been understood. Skilled customer service managers know that by repeating what an angry customer is saying, they can reduce the level of hostility. Remaining calm while doing so sends a message about your own professionalism and poise.

Before expressing apologies, before solving a problem, let the person know that they have been heard by repeating the specifics:

- *"So I can expect the budget changes by Thursday?"*

- *"We agree you plan on issuing the invitation via snail mail?"*

- *"You and I will revisit this during our next meeting, that works for you?"*

- *"Just so I am sure I understand you, your food was not delivered on time and it was cold?"*

- *"I understand you wish to make our relationship exclusive sooner rather than later, or are you saying something else?"*

- *"If I sponsor this organization, I will receive the following . . . correct?"*

Ten Tips for Tip-Top Listening

1. Learn to want to listen. You must have the desire, interest, concentration, and self-discipline.

2. To be a good listener, give verbal and visual cues that you are listening.

3. Anticipate excellence. We get good information more often when we expect it.

4. Become a "whole body" listener. Listen with your ears, your eyes, and your heart.

5. Take notes. They aid retention.

6. Listen now, report later. Plan to tell someone what you heard, and you will remember it better.

7. Build rapport by pacing the speaker. Approximate the speaker's gestures, facial expressions, and voice patterns to create comfortable communication.

8. Control internal and external distractions.

9. Generously give the gift of listening.

10. Be present, beware the tendency to daydream or multitask. Don't drift off from conversations.

MENTAL LISTENING SKILLS

All the visual and verbal cues in the world are useless if you haven't stayed focused enough on the conversation to track it well. A good conversation partner retains what's been said. If you are too bored to stay with the conversation, exit gracefully instead of embarrassing your conversation partner by demonstrating boredom.

I had a business lunch with a woman who shall remain nameless. I told her a story about my kids and mentioned that my second and current husband is a periodontist. Several minutes later, during a pause in the conversation, she asked if I was married! Clearly, she had drifted away in the conversation.

Don't jeopardize a relationship by failing to listen. Your job as a conversation partner is to listen when the other person is speaking. This isn't optional—it's a required courtesy when conversing. If, for whatever reason, you cannot remain focused on what the speaker is saying, excuse yourself. The messages you send through visual, verbal, and mental cues let your partner know the status of the conversation. If you feel trapped in a conversation and don't know how to exit, read on. We'll take care of that dilemma as well.

7

PREVENT PREGNANT PAUSES
WITH PREPARATION

Even with icebreakers, conversation-makers, and active listening, there are still times when the conversation can grind to a halt if you're not prepared. Invariably, at any conference luncheon, at least one table of eight intelligent people ends up staring at their plates trying to figure out how to get the conversation rolling after they've "talked shop" ten minutes too long! They could have avoided extensive examination of the rice pilaf if just one person had been prepared. Yes, prepared—as in advance planning.

All eight knew they would be sitting down with seven people they didn't know. A good conversationalist prepares before the event. No worries—slides, laptop presentations, and laser pointers are not required! All that is needed is a bit of forethought that can be accomplished in the car on the way to the event. Here are a few foolproof ideas:

Jump Starters

- Did anyone happen to catch that special playoff game last night?
- Have any of you seen the film . . . ?
- I just finished reading _____. Has anyone read it yet?
- Have any of you heard of that new _____ app?
- Will someone explain cryptocurrency to me?
- Does anyone here have a (bank, hair stylist, stockbroker, etc.) they could recommend?
- How has Zoom impacted your world?
- Tell me about love in your life . . .

A favorite jump starter before a virtual meeting is called to order is, *Where are you today?* Working from home is a new normal. However, home can be in a childhood home, a shared workspace, an entirely different city or town thanks to the quickly changing landscape of work. Responses to *Where are you?* can range from "in my kitchen," to "moved to New Orleans," to "a few days with my sister in Kansas City," to "the airport." Or take advantage of observing free information resources looking for pictures, trophies, snow falling, and fake backgrounds to start a conversation.

DON'T LET OLD ACQUAINTANCES BE FORGOTTEN

You need more than icebreakers to enjoy your time conversing with others. You need to tailor your preparation to the nature of the occasion and the people with whom you'll be talking. One of the toughest audiences—after kids—is an acquaintance you see only once in a while. You have some history together, you know a bit about each other, and you don't have a clue what's changed in the year since you last saw each other. In fact, it's good to assume that things probably have changed. Suppose you check in with a colleague annually for an industry function. In the past twelve months your colleague may have gotten a different job, experienced the death of a close friend or relative, gone on an extraordinary vacation, had a spiritual awakening, or gotten married or divorced. In other words, don't presume that you are picking up a conversation that started a year ago. Without asking *So what's new?*, a question that begs the conversation-stopping answer *Not much*, seek out what's new and keep the conversation rolling with questions like these:

With Acquaintances Use . . .

- Bring me up to date on . . .
- What's been going on with work since I last saw you?
- What has changed in your life since we spoke last?
- Bring me up to date on your child's post-high school plans . . .
- How's your year been?
- What's new with the family?
- Catch me up on the project . . .

With Acquaintances Don't Use . . .

- How's your wife/husband/partner/spouse?
- How's your job at . . . ?
- Did your daughter get asked to prom?
- How are the wedding plans going?

- Any babies in the future?
- What are your child's college plans?
- Did she graduate?

All of the above can backfire if you do not know the person well.

And never ask a Texan, acquaintance or not, *What's the size of your spread?*

GETTING A HISTORY LESSON

Frequently, you find yourself in an awkward silence or a pregnant pause in the conversation. It is up to you to either invigorate the conversation or allow it to slowly grind to a halt. Do your part to charge up the conversation by being prepared with questions on the origin and history of those people you are with. For instance, you can inquire:

History Lessons

- How did you two meet?
- How did you get started _____?

History Lessons

- What got you interested in this area?
- When did you first know you wanted to be a
  _____?
- What brought you to Colorado?
- How do you all know each other?
- What got you interested in marketing?
- What gave you the idea for this business?
- What happened first?

When you ask the fellow with your boss, *How do you know each other?* you may learn he's the boss's new husband. Or instead his brother, colleague, or friend. Never make assumptions that folks are or are not together romantically. Give them the rope they need to respond in whatever way works best for them.

PREPARING FOR THE LONG HAUL

Prepare for a conversation like you'd prepare for an interview—both as the interviewer and the interviewee. It takes much less effort to prepare for a conversation than a job interview, but the philosophy is the same. You want to have material prepared that is relevant to the event or interaction so that you can converse articulately and gracefully. I call the questions that fall into this category "interviewing questions"; they help keep the conversation humming along. As I drive into a parking lot before entering a meeting, luncheon, or any type of function, or as I click on the link to be connected, or ready for a planned phone call, I prepare as if for an interview. I spend two minutes thinking about specific interviewing questions that apply to the person(s), event, or situation I am about to encounter. Most of us find ourselves seated across from a stranger we know nothing about, speaking with a fellow parent on the phone for the first time, or about to click the link for a first-time virtual meeting with a prospect, doctor, date, or fellow church volunteer; we panic and cannot think of anything to say. What an awkward moment! Think about it: When is the worst time to think of something to talk about? When there is nothing to talk about! Here are some examples of interviewing questions you can customize to fit your own personality:

Interviewing Questions

- What do you enjoy most about this season of the year?
- What got you involved in this organization/event?
- If you weren't here, what would you be doing at this very moment?
- If you could meet any one person, whom would you choose?
- Tell me about an issue that matters a great deal to you.
- What has been your most important work experience?
- How is your day going?
- What is your greatest challenge as a parent?
- What do you like about virtual dating?
- What is the weather like where you are?

When you are getting together with a person you have spent time with before, review some of the particulars you learned on previous occasions. Maybe you discussed the M.B.A. they were working on, or the volleyball league they coach each spring, or the fact that gardening is a beloved hobby. Don't expect to recall these specifics during a pregnant pause. Instead, prepare yourself!

Interviewing Questions

- What word would you say describes you best?
- Do you have a personal motto or creed?
- Do you have any heroes that you greatly admire?
- What did people in high school think you were like?
- What's on your bucket list?
- If you could go back to your teenage self, what would your advice be?
- What two things can you not live without?
- What are you most proud of?
- What is the number one ingredient to your success? What is your secret sauce?
- What do you do that you wish you could stop doing?

THE NONVERBAL PART OF THE CONVERSATION

One of my favorite exercises when teaching Small Talk seminars illustrates the point beautifully. I get ten to twelve people in a circle and arbitrarily hand one of them a ball of yarn. That person must hold on to the end of the yarn, disclose something about herself, and toss the ball of yarn to someone else in the group. The recipient must ask a question of the thrower about what she said. The recipient must then tell something about himself, hold on to the string, and toss the ball of yarn to the next person. This continues until every person has had the ball.

I love this exercise because the participants discover several things. First, since they don't know when they'll receive the ball, they truly listen to what everyone else says. Paying attention is the only way they'll be able to ask an intelligent question. Second, they learn to focus on asking *appropriate, related questions or making appropriate, related verbal cues.* Asking appropriate questions and making appropriate comments is one of the easiest ways to keep the conversation chugging seamlessly along. Last, they pay attention to body language, because the speaker always makes eye contact prior to throwing, so that the ball won't be dropped! If the speaker doesn't make eye contact or the listener isn't paying attention, the conversation abruptly ends with a noticeable thud.

Advance planning helps ensure that the ball doesn't get dropped. If you are at an event where you'll spend a considerable amount of time with the same group, such as a luncheon, party, or conference, be prepared to move beyond icebreakers and initial conversation-makers. You need to be prepared to engage in longer conversations, so you need more topics. This needn't be difficult. If you are worried that you'll forget, keep a cheat sheet in your wallet or on your device to peruse just prior to lunch.

The one topic that you needn't have a list for is the one you know best: yourself. Out of courtesy to the introverts in the crowd, I have waited until we were well into the book before getting to this point. Regardless of how many appropriate questions you have on hand, sooner or later you must talk about yourself. The rules of good conversation require give and take. If you only ask questions, your conversation partner will resent the lack of parity. It's important that each person tell about themselves. This is a stretch for some people, though. It used to be a stretch for me, too. I have discovered that most people who are reticent to talk about themselves fear one or both of the following:

1. They worry that their lives are too ordinary to be interesting.
2. They do not want to appear self-centered or conceited.

ORDINARY PEOPLE

Guess what? Most of us are ordinary people just trying to live our lives. We worry about paying bills, educating kids, our favorite team winning a championship, getting a promotion, caring for elderly parents, taking an occasional vacation, having time for a hobby, and relaxing now and then. We are more alike than we are different, and our commonality as human beings opens the door for connection and conversation. Even ordinary people have extraordinary things happen to them that make for excellent conversation. Every person I know has had an extraordinary experience of one kind or another. Lurking somewhere in your conversation is a hilarious event, a once-in-a-lifetime vacation, a ridiculous moment, an exciting accomplishment, a hair-raising happy-ending tale, an uncanny coincidence, or an incredible adventure. Find it and bring it out! Almost anything is a conversation in the making.

LIMELIGHT ETIQUETTE

There are a few rules to remember as you reluctantly step into the limelight. You will do fine if you follow this advice—no one is skulking about with a hook looking to pull you offstage. First, disclose information about yourself that is comfortable and uncontroversial. Lead with easy, positive, and light information. Building trust and intimacy over time creates friendships and fosters business relationships. Having a conversation is a little like peeling an onion—you want to proceed in layers, matching the level of intimacy shared by your partner.

For instance, suppose your small-talking sidekick has just confessed that, after a long holdout, the realities of being a soccer parent resulted in their family buying a minivan. This does not open the door for you to say that you've been recently diagnosed with breast cancer. However, if the conversation were taking place at the Race for the Cure, and you were wearing a pink ribbon indicating that you were a cancer survivor, it would be acceptable to discuss breast cancer. Your choice of conversation material should be appropriate to the occasion and to the depth of rapport and intimacy established.

I recently attended a luncheon where I was seated at one of those round tables with seven people I had never met. We came to a lull in the conversation that instantly made everyone decide it was time to look at their personal devices for messages. I assumed the burden of conversation and jumped in with a story about a vacation that my family had taken over spring break. I said, *We went on a Club Med vacation in Mexico last spring and had a great time. It was so hassle-free I couldn't believe it. Since you pay a flat fee for everything, I didn't have to fish for money every time the kids wanted a Coke. They just went and got it. It seemed so effortless, and there were activities for all of us.*

My vacation story accomplished three things that rejuvenated the conversation. First, I told something about myself, giving others the opportunity to feel more connected to me. Increasing that comfort level stimulates conversation. Second, I offered a new topic that gave material for the others to use. Third, it gave my tablemates the chance to share their own experiences. Our conversation sprang to life immediately, as others jumped in with questions, stories, and vacation plans of their own. Being willing to disclose first is assuming the burden of the conversation and the reward is others will model your disclosure with their own. You aren't limited to talking about events and experiences. You can share feelings, opinions about books you've read, restaurants you've visited, and movies you've seen. For instance, I was at an awards banquet talking with a gentleman. He said, *I'm really nervous being here. My wife had to go away on business so I'm here alone, and I don't know anyone else.* I talked with him about how nervous I used to get at social functions. That brief exchange helped calm him, and we went on to converse at length about a variety of topics.

Speak No Evil

Barring exceptional circumstances, avoid these often-controversial topics that can stop a conversation in its tracks:

1. Stories of questionable taste
2. Gossip
3. Personal misfortunes, particularly current ones
4. How much things cost!
5. Controversial subjects when you don't know where people stand
6. Health (yours or theirs). The exception is when you're talking with a person who has an obvious new cast, crutches, or bandage. In that situation, the apparent temporary medical apparatus is free information. If you skirt the issue, it's a bit like having an elephant in your living room and ignoring it.

While there is an infinite list of acceptable conversation topics at public venues, there is also a short list of subjects that are generally off-limits. If you are unsure about a subject's appropriateness and hesitate before bringing it up, it's probably better left unspoken. When unsure, I always invoke the old math axiom my algebra teacher taught me: *When in doubt, leave it out.* Avoid any area that is likely to offend your conversation partner.

PLAYING FOURSQUARE

Keeping a conversation rolling is not unlike the old playground game of foursquare. You must pass the ball among all the players and keep the ball inbounds for play to continue. This requires focusing on the ball at all times and passing it around. Some of the people in your group may be reluctant to receive the ball for the same reasons that you were—they're shy, feel like their lives are too ordinary, don't enjoy the attention, et cetera. It's up to you to help them, or the game will fall apart.

One of the easiest ways to start or keep a conversation going is to compliment another person. Finding something nice to say about someone is usually not that difficult. Surely they have something to like about them. Being forthright enough to tell them what you admire about them makes an immediate connection between the two of you. With connection comes its etymological cousin, conversation. An authentic compliment makes the other person feel good about both of you, and that enhances the rapport, making conversation easier. The key is that your compliment is genuine, so select something that you can truly support. No matter what you choose, it will fall into one of these three categories: appearance, possessions, or behavior. Mark Twain once said that a good compliment lasted him sixty days!

Prior to my wedding, I had a conversation with my good friend Karen about all the arrangements. I told her that for a period of time, I had been seeing two men—Ben and Steve. She invited me to tell her about both of them. I said, *Ben has a great sense of humor. He's the life of the party. He dresses like a million bucks and has taken me on wonderful trips. We've been to Hilton Head, Europe, and had a bunch of weekend mountain getaways. He's a great golfer and an all-around wonderful guy.*

Karen could hardly contain herself, she was so excited. She said, *He sounds like a dream. I'm so happy that you're marrying him.*

I'm not, I replied. *I'm marrying Steve.*

Karen was speechless. Finally, she collected herself and said, *Well Debra, Ben sounds like a prince. Why are you marrying Steve?*

Because he makes me feel so special because of all the wonderful things he says about me. And you know what? He means every one of them!

The power in a sincere compliment is enormous. There is nothing that makes people feel more special than to have their finer traits noted and appreciated.

THE PERFECT COMPLIMENT

You can compliment someone on a new hairstyle, an item of clothing, a piece of jewelry, or physical appearance. However, not all compliments are created equal. A good compliment acknowledges the object of admiration: *That's a nice sweater you're wearing* or *What an unusual tie.* An excellent, top-of-the-line compliment goes beyond that to give *conversation material* by expounding on why you like the item. For instance, you might elaborate on the sweater by saying, *I love your sweater. That shade really enhances the color of your eyes.* You can turn your appreciation of a good-looking tie into a more powerful compliment by saying, *That's a great tie. Its unusual design really sets it apart, I always enjoy it when men make fashion statements with their ties.* Beware of complimenting appearance in the workplace. In many instances it can be construed as a form of sexual harassment.

Perhaps you are with someone who has no fashion sense whatsoever, and you have no appreciation for her taste in clothing, makeup, or accessories. Fear not—you may do better in complimenting her on a possession such as her home, an elegant fountain pen, a new car, even a coffee mug. A good compliment would be: *You have a lovely home.* Turn that into state-of-the-art flattery by saying: *Your home is lovely. I really like all the photos you have—they personalize your home and give it a lot of warmth.* Instead of saying, *This is a great cup of coffee*, consider, *I love the richness of Indonesian Sumatra, and this is a great-size mug.* Be sure to take note of all the above when meeting virtually. Look for awards, pictures, framed slogans, and plants. Some backgrounds are so gorgeous and cozy they turn out to be fake! Which will bring lots of laughs.

Last but not least, you can notice and compliment someone else's behavior. This is the best way to converse with kids. Instead of noticing when they do something wrong, try celebrating positive behavior. It'll go a long way toward furthering communication with them and deepening your bond. Kids aren't the only ones who appreciate compliments regarding their behavior. Adults can really open up in the wake of such acknowledgment.

My daughter Sarah, a Realtor, took a couple house-hunting one Sunday. She drove them all over town and probably showed them over thirty houses. They went in and out of neighborhoods in town, in the suburbs—the works. After six hours, they had completely run out of things to say and still hadn't found a single house that the couple was remotely considering. The Realtor was tired and just about out of ideas. Then she said, *I really admire that you know exactly what you want. You're not going to settle for something that you don't want and then possibly be unhappy with your choice later.* That one compliment got the couple charged up again and they were able to find a new topic of conversation to get them through the day, although they didn't locate their dream house that Sunday. Other behavioral compliments include comments like:

- I appreciate how organized you are for our meetings. It makes it easy to get the work done.

- It must have taken a lot of courage to change careers during your peak of success. I really admire that.

- You have an amazing amount of determination. I think it's remarkable that you set aside time to successfully train for a marathon. Congratulations.

- I know you are nervous about this procedure; it's great that you made yourself show up.

- You certainly look at the bright side of things; it is a pleasure to work with you.

- You manage to run such an organized home, even with four children!

Again, the ticket to a successful pat on the back is that you offer it sincerely. You may find that the person you are complimenting has difficulty receiving the praise. He may try to neutralize the compliment by denying it or feel obligated to return a compliment. If that happens, reaffirm your sincerity and move on to another subject.

ADDING FORM AND SUBSTANCE

Besides complimenting the other person, another way to draw a reluctant speaker into the conversation is to toss her the ball by asking a question. In addition to the ice-breakers back in Chapter 2, there are four categories of questions that are effective in social situations. I use the acronym FORM to remember them:

Family

Tell me about your family.

Does everyone live in the area?

What do you like best about being a father/mother/son/aunt, et cetera?

Occupation

What got you into your current job?

How did you come up with that idea?

What are some of the toughest challenges in your work?

If you could change one thing about your job, what would it be?

How has social media impacted your business/industry?

Recreation

What do you do for fitness?

What kinds of things does your family do for fun?

How do you spend your leisure time?

What's been your favorite vacation?

Miscellaneous

Have you seen any good movies lately?

What do you think about _____ {news event}?

Are you reading anything you really enjoy?

No matter what your chosen topic of conversation, I cannot overstate the importance of being authentic when talking with someone. If you are not genuinely interested in what the other person is saying, no amount of planning or preparation will save you from a doomed conversation. Interest in someone else cannot be feigned. If you truly cannot muster any enthusiasm for the dialogue, you owe it to your partner to excuse yourself and make your way to another approachable person.

THE MARCH OF PROGRESS

You are well into this book. By now you've become familiar with techniques to make you an excellent conversationalist. It's a good time to reflect on how far you've come as you practice these skills and identify the opportunities for improvement that lay before you. Take the "Winning at Small Talk" quiz again and see if you've made any improvement. Look yourself in the mirror and respond with honest "yes" or "no" answers to the following statements:

- I'm conscious of taking turns in conversations so that I can find out about others and help them get to know me.

- I have joined or participated in at least one club or group activity in order to develop new business or social friendships.

- I have used my contacts to help at least two people find new jobs or hook up with potential customers and clients. I have given information to someone for other networking purposes.

- I attend either virtually or face-to-face at least two functions a month where I can meet people in my profession/industry or who share a common interest.

- If another person is friendly to me, I find it easy to be friendly back. However, I don't wait to make sure the other person is friendly before I'm friendly in return.

- When someone asks *What's new?*, instead of saying *Not much*, I often talk about something exciting in my life.

- During virtual meetings I jump in to say hello, not waiting to be formally introduced. Unless activity in my office or personal circumstances do not allow for a live video, I do not go dark. I demonstrate positive body language, good eye contact, and genuine interest.

How did you do? If you're like me, you probably still have some work to do. It takes effort and practice to change habits. I suggest that you write down one statement reflecting what you want to conquer. Focus on that one goal until you feel comfortable, and then move on to the next. When you stay focused, it won't take long! A simple rule that garners great rewards is to start conversations with a minimum of three new people a week—with someone in line at the grocery, with a coworker while waiting for a meeting to begin, with your next-door neighbor. I spoke earlier of turning new interactions into tasks. Tackle meeting new people or renewing acquaintances as a task that you schedule at least three times a week. Comfort will come with steady practice. Along with the rewards that result.

8

CONVERSATIONAL CLOUT

I do not suggest that you use aggressive conversation tactics; however, I do propose that you use assertive, rather than passive, language. Allow your conversation methods to convey your core strength. How many times do we hear words come out of our mouths that sound meek, apologetic, and hesitant? When you offer to *try to get back to you by tomorrow*, you are admitting that a firm expectation does not exist. The words we select for conversation can convey messages we do not intend to deliver. Has a member of the wait staff at a restaurant ever said to you *We can't make substitutions* or a customer service representative responded to your inquiry with *If I can find out . . . ?* As you will discover in this chapter, certain expressions and statements, as well as questions, can lead the conversation down an unintended path. Be aware when you use the following examples and notice how you project yourself in the course of conversation.

- *When will that be ready?* Put yourself in the driver's seat.
  Instead: *Will you please have that ready for me by Tuesday?*

- *I'd hate to direct you to the wrong store.* Hate to do what? Hate to make a mistake?
  Instead: *I do not know what store to direct you to.* Or, *I believe that you can find that product at _____.*

- *I was going to say that property taxes seem high* and *I would think that roses would require more sunshine than this space provides.* This qualifies what you are about to say. Either statement sounds cautious and timid.
  Instead: *I believe property taxes are high* or *From my experience, roses require more sunshine than is provided in this space.*

- *Can I interrupt you for a minute? Can I ask you a question?* You already have! If you are willing to

interrupt someone when they are engaged, just ask
the question! But to be polite, you could offer *I'm
sorry to interrupt . . .* and then ask your question.

- *I'll have to ask someone about that . . .* Who are you?
No one?
Instead: *I'll be glad to check with accounting and get
back to you.*

- *I'll be honest with you, I had a great time!* Aren't you
always honest? Are you qualifying this particular
statement over others you have made?
Instead: *I had a great time!*

- *Can you spell your name for me?* Most of us know how
to spell our names, we do not need to be asked first
if we know how!
Instead: *Please spell your name for me.*

- *If I can find out . . .* A low expectation is established
when you use the word *if.* Raise expectations. Instill
confidence.
Instead: *I will look into this and get back to you one
way or the other.*

- *I'm only the . . .* Everyone's role or job is important. This is demeaning to oneself. Define the capabilities and responsibilities in your area of expertise.
  Instead: *My responsibilities are focused on website development. I will be glad to check with sales about your order.*

- *I can't meet with you this morning.* This projects an unwillingness to deliver the best possible outcome. Or it projects a burden. Tell them what you can do.
  Instead: *I can be there by three this afternoon.*

- *I'll try to get this back to you this week.* The word *try* conveys the underlying message that this is not something that is dependable.
  Instead: *I'll get to you no later than next week.* Tell people what you will do, not what you hope to do.

- *I'll have to . . .* Another burden. *I'll have to check with my husband* or *I'll have to check with my team.*
  Instead: *I'll be glad to check with my husband* and *I'll be glad to speak to my team and get back to you.*

- *You'll have to call me tomorrow. This is a busy time for me.* This sounds like a person giving orders and placing another burden on my already heavy load! And I don't like to be bossed around.
  Instead: *You can call me tomorrow. That's a better time for me.*

- *I'm really not too sure.* Yes, you are sure. You are sure you don't know!
  Instead: *I don't know how to get to Colfax. Ask Jennifer. She is good with directions.*

- *May I ask your name?* Permission is not necessary to ask someone's name!
  Instead: *What is your name?*

We are what we say, and the true window to our souls is our words. Let your words bespeak the strength within.

9

CRIMES AND MISDEMEANORS

I travel frequently, small talking my way across the country. One of the biggest trends I've seen is an increase in "assault on a conversation with a deadly weapon." I've been victimized myself a couple of times. You should know that these people are armed and dangerous, and if they enter your dialogue, you are at serious risk of witnessing the torturous murder of your conversation. Stay on your toes; these people are cleverly disguised. They can orchestrate several costume changes at a single event and impersonate people in every profession. If you sense danger, stay calm. Be on the lookout for these renegades. One further cautionary note: Often, the worst offenders are staring back at us from the mirror.

I've decided it's time to get more aggressive in preventing conversational crimes. I've investigated this phenomenon extensively and have organized the killers into eight classifications. During the course of your own daily conversation, try not to add your own name to the Conversational Criminals Most Wanted list. Here are some crime-fighting techniques to keep honest conversationalists safe.

THE FBI AGENT

The FBI agent definitely does not have the national interest at heart. He or she can be seen stalking casual conversations and pulling people aside for interrogation. You will immediately recognize their unmistakable modus operandi because they fire question after question at you, like a machine gun in a jungle. *What do you do for a living? Where are you from? You married? Got any kids? Lived here long? How long have you been on the job? What's your mother's maiden name?*

Notice that the FBI agent relentlessly assaults his captive with a barrage of questions. He leaves no opportunity for his captive to offer a confession of any kind. The captive is not allowed to expand, offer additional evidence, ask questions, or even have a glass of water. Forget about

The FBI agent

making a phone call or getting a lawyer. The captive is forced to give staccato answers just to keep pace. He is held in custody at the whim of the interrogator, who, when finished with the questioning, unceremoniously dumps the captive and moves on to round up another suspect.

The interrogatory method seldom works to anyone's satisfaction. The agent would be much more successful if he asked open-ended questions requiring more extensive answers. The detainee would cough up plenty of information effortlessly if given the opportunity. The agent also makes the mistake of settling for one- or two-word answers. Digging deeper could have uncovered motives, alibis, opportunities, and background information that would have proved quite helpful in the agent's quest for conversation had he asked appropriate, probing questions. He misses a great opportunity to gain information by not confessing something about himself first, which might have caused you to drop your guard and be more at ease, turning the interrogation into a conversation.

The FBI agent is characterized by his exceptional nervousness. Help this person out by taking control of the conversational ball. Ask him an open-ended question. Follow up—dig deeper and use verbal listening cues. For instance, ask him to describe a typical day. Follow up with questions about what that kind of job entails and how he got into it. Become the host and attend to his comfort. This will allow you to slow down the conversation. Eventually you'll ease into a nice rhythm, a back-and-forth volley with the conversational ball.

THE BRAGGART

This convict made his way onto the Most Wanted list by executing a series of conversational mass murders in almost every state. He frequently appears during periods of self-disclosure. He will boast of his accomplishments, embellish the truth, and brag about feats mighty and small in a very self-aggrandizing manner. He usually makes no attempt to go incognito, so arrogant is he. His goal is to gain status in the eyes of those in attendance, so he welcomes an audience. The bigger the group, the more bravado he feels. He has been known to kill multiple conversations with a single appearance.

His trademark is that he will always relate all of his accomplishments. He made a killing in the stock market. He'll tell how he outwitted the financial experts by choosing a long shot that paid off big. Of course, his son is the captain of the baseball team, and pro scouts are recruiting the boy. He'll spare you no details. Perhaps he just bought a top-of-the-line gizmo. He can't imagine why everyone else doesn't do the same. He always has an "I'm king of the world" story to tell.

The braggart's sister, Braggarita, is equally lethal, although she prefers single encounters with people she knows. She usually prefers to do her boasting in a more personal way. She tends to speak conspiratorially to members of her inner circle. She leaves it to them to spread the word of Braggarita's greatness to unknown parties. Braggarita never directly discloses her greatness to strangers. She lets them find out from her coterie of confidantes who are charged with telling others. While strangers are not required to bow to Braggarita, it is expected that they will be suitably impressed.

She will very quietly tell her inner circle about her new designer kitchen and how much it cost. She'll tell them about a smashing vacation on the French Riviera that everyone else must take. In fact, she'll give you the name of her travel agent just so you can replicate the trip. She will ask you if your daughter was asked to prom, only so that she can crow about her own daughter's triumph.

Either of these lawless conversationalists are sure to whip out their phones to show pictures of their darling grandchildren, handsome graduate, or perfect bride. Without a touch of shame, they may even continue to scroll. Yikes!

The only hope of stopping a small-talk murder orchestrated by the braggart and Braggarita is to bring the conversation back to more general topics, such as current events. You can also refocus the conversation on your own life, telling about something that you are currently doing. There is no point in going toe-to-toe with either of them, because it is impossible to directly stave off their boastfulness. Your only weapon is redirecting the conversation.

CAN YOU TOP THIS? (THE ONE-UPPER)

Members of this long-standing conversational crime family are first cousins to the braggart and his sister. These folks generally come from a patriarchal lineage, as women have a slightly different method to their murder. While the one-uppers generally do not brag first, they always top someone else's story. They seem to be completely unaware that they have offended other small talkers by constantly trumping another person's story. Sometimes the one-uppers genuinely believe they are showing compassion and demonstrating excellent listening skills by topping another's tale.

You know the scene. Your colleague Brian is looking for a new job, and you inquire about how the search is progressing. As soon as Brian offers an update, John launches into a tale about his own difficulties on the job, making it seem like unemployment is preferable to his own job woes. Before you know it, the group is talking all about what's going on in the industry, and Brian's job search is lost in the shuffle. His troubles aren't acknowledged. No solutions are offered. No sympathy is given. No encouraging words found him. Brian is left feeling like no one really cares about his plight. While John might have thought he was being supportive, he wasn't. He simply diverted attention away from Brian and onto himself.

Women are experts at topping another's story, but their approach is to match someone else's. For instance, Rose talks about relationship problems she's having with Steven, and Shelley commiserates by saying, *Honey, I know just what you mean. My Anthony had the nerve to* . . . The woman who topped the initial woman's story didn't really commiserate. She stole the show. She took the spotlight off the other woman and put it right on herself. She stopped the other woman in the middle of her story.

A business friend, Vivian, recounted the following horror story she and her beau witnessed at a swinging soiree in Washington, DC: "Another couple attended with us. During the reception, the wife—we'll call her Cathy—commented that another woman who was standing nearby had on the same 'outfit' that she was wearing. As the woman approached, Cathy struck up a conversation. Cathy commented on how they were wearing the same gown (actually, the outfits were similar but not exactly the same). Anyway, Cathy then asked this woman, whom she had just met, where she bought her outfit. The woman told her the name of a well-known, expensive store. I could not believe the next words out of Cathy's mouth. 'Oh, I got mine at a thrift shop for fifteen dollars!' "

A particularly troublesome spot for women is talking about their kids. Sometimes I have to fight myself to keep from jumping in and telling my own kid tales when another woman is telling a story about hers. Instead of enjoying the story she is sharing, I can get sidetracked, because her story reminds me of something similar that my kids did at that age. I get so excited that I just want to jump right in there because I'm exhilarated by the conversation. This is not a stalled conversation—this is one in which everyone wants the ball! However, it's very deflating to the person telling the original story. Her story is the one that got the group so enthusiastic. It's important to acknowledge that and to enjoy such a great story. There's no need to rush to the next. It's like hurrying through a glass of fine wine—you miss most of the experience in the rush to complete it! Stay focused on other people and their stories. We do seek commonality. Without so much as a cautionary yellow light, we jump in to match similar experiences. Yes, there is a time to share, and sometimes holding one's tongue can be torture although ultimately less painful then committing another conversation killer. Take the few minutes to truly listen; the truth is, we all know our own stories, what we do not know is other people's life, work, and recreational experiences. After a few minutes, share your commonality and keep the conversation volleying back and forth.

Be aware of one of the most prevalent one-upping statements circulating these days: *Been there, done that.* In one very short sentence, the person uttering those four words is saying that the story is old news, that there is nothing else to say about that topic. It lets the other person know, in no uncertain terms, that their experience is universal and he can spare the rest of us the details of such a boring story. Crime stoppers report that it is tough to topple the one-upper, who is quite successful in crushing the conversation to death. Those still standing usually attempt to regroup in a clandestine fashion to prevent another crime.

Lindsay is a great person, but in her attempts to relate, she's sometimes guilty of being a one-upper. Too many times when someone is sharing the details of an experience, she will interrupt to say, essentially, *Oh yes, that happened to me, too . . .* She confessed to me that her friend Judy was telling the story about her vacation to South America. They were on the Amazon River, when a huge scorpion bit a woman in their party. Lindsay broke in: "I was on a river in Kansas once, and the daddy longlegs were as big as your hat!" Judy patted her arm and said, "Lindsay, this is my story."

THE MONOPOLIZER

A master of disguise, the monopolizer has managed to infiltrate conversations across the globe. Despite the all-too-common shout of "Unmute yourself!" along with the ability to handily use the mute button during virtual meetings, there is not yet an invention to mute the monopolizer on the phone or in person. Victims are shocked to discover that even a very introverted or shy person can turn out to be a monopolizer. Many social media posts are unfortunate examples of the longwinded offender assuming that others will have interest in their litany of complaints, concerns, or opinions. Thankfully, social media can be ignored or turned off. However, the monopolizer can turn up anywhere, even at the most exclusive of events. They strike boldly, seizing the conversation in plain view of all. They can enter any conversation and artfully gain control before a single person can react. There is never any shortage of witnesses to the monopolizer's crimes; nevertheless, people are initially too captivated to take action. The monopolizer takes the spotlight through self-disclosure and retains it by continuing to "peel the layers of the onion" without regard to whether anyone in the group is feeling any discomfort.

Monopolizers feel justified: They believe they are performing a community service by keeping the conversational ball rolling. Usually shy people who find that the spotlight is rather fun can be the worst offenders. A shy person who garners interest in her recent dedication to yoga or her new role as a managing director throws caution to the wind, resulting in a twelve-minute soliloquy. Instead of hogging the ball, the monopolizer should pass it to someone else in the group. I have a personal rule that I never talk for more than five minutes before passing the ball. Time can fly when we are talking about ourselves! No matter what the topic—how I launched my business or met my second husband, how I got into business, why my kids are so incredible—the clock is ticking. When my five minutes are up, I pass the ball to someone else with an appropriate question or comment. It's not just our golfing buddies or in-laws who are monopolizers! Look in the mirror, make sure it's not you! Don't get me started! (Another overworked expression of our times.)

If you are alone with a monopolizer, you have several options to salvage the situation. If you are with your boss, a client, or your mother-in-law, it's usually best to surrender and give the gift of listening. Once in a while you can be successful for brief interludes by changing the topic, using self-disclosure, or asking a prepared question. However, it is impossible to make a monopolizer stop. You can't change another person. If your career or your relationship with your extended family is on the line, just surrender and consider it a random act of kindness.

There are occasions when you can successfully stop a monopolizer. When you are approaching your saturation point, throw out a white flag as a warning. Just like a race car driver gets a white flag indicating time constraints, you must throw one before you can legitimately stop a monopolizer in his tracks. For example: You are in your office, and your colleague Gary comes by to tell you about his golf game. When you are running out of time, interest, or willpower, you throw a white flag by saying, *Wow, Gary. That's an amazing round you shot. Before you continue, I need to let you know that in a few minutes I have to get back to preparing the budget.* You have politely given Gary the signal that you need to end the conversation shortly. Gary takes another four minutes telling you of his exploits on the twelfth and thirteenth holes. You can now wrap it up by saying, *Well, Gary, that's really something. I have to take care of the budget right now. Maybe we can catch up another time.* You can now turn your attention to your budget without worry. You were gracious and obliging, and you gave fair warning that it was time to end the chat.

If you are in a group of three or more, assume the role of host and make an interception. Every year I get together to catch up with some college friends for an evening. My friend Lori is infamous for her legendary ability to monopolize the conversation. Given my line of work, I feel obligated to help the group and facilitate passing the ball. So I jump in after she's had more than her five minutes on the floor and say, *Lori, that's a great story about Adam's hitting streak. Marilyn, what's been going on with your kids?* Connecting Lori's story about her son to Marilyn's kids lends continuity to the conversation while diplomatically allowing someone else a chance to talk. As Uncle Joe is going on endlessly about the life of an auditor, transition the conversation to someone else. *That sounds tough, Uncle Joe. Cousin Larry, what's going on for you at work?*

Monopolizers have shown that they are candidates for rehabilitation. They have been successful in restoring conversational balance once they realize that talking incessantly is not exactly a favor to everyone else.

Remember, assuming the burden as the host, your goal is not only to get the monopolizer to yield the floor, it is to include others—especially the quiet ones. Invite them into the dialogue with a question or comment directed to them. Even when there isn't a monopolizer in the conversation, pass the ball to everyone.

THE INTERRUPTER

Beware the interrupter! This villain comes in all shapes, sizes, and haircuts. I've often wondered if the interrupter was prevented from ever finishing a sentence as a kid and is retaliating against society. The interrupter is characterized by high drive, determination to make her point, and a lack of patience. I confess that I have done time as an interrupter. I was convicted of interrupting my husband relentlessly. I was on probation for a while, but after three strikes, I was in the joint. My husband is very low-key, and my conviction caused him a great deal of angst. He understood my temperament and was torn about confronting me. But after I interrupted him one too many times, he demanded justice.

Frequently, he would start to say something and provide rationale for his point. If I didn't agree, I'd jump right in without letting him finish. I didn't want to wait three minutes for him to make his case. It was an eternity. Most interrupters are like me. We interrupt because we think we know what you're going to say, so let's not waste time. Or we know that you are wrong, and we must hurry to point out the errors in your thinking.

However, having already gone through one divorce, I wasn't interested in destroying our near-perfect union with my short attention span and lack of patience. I have since realized that interruptions badly sabotage a good conversation, so now I campaign against them. There are only three good reasons for interrupting. The first is that you need to exit immediately. The second is that the topic of conversation is too uncomfortable to bear, and you need to change the subject right away. And the third is if you are in the company of a monopolizer who has refused to offer you a natural break in the conversation for more than five minutes.

THE POOR SPORT

The poor sport has an unparalleled reputation for small-talk suicide. The poor sport will kill their own conversation by refusing to play by the rules. A very cunning illusion artist, the poor sport changes open-ended questions into closed-end quips. Using smoke and mirrors, the poor sport always finds a way to reduce a beautiful question into a simple one-word answer. When asked *What did you do this weekend?*, the poor sport will reply with *Nothing*. The question left plenty of room for the poor sport to select some aspect of the weekend for conversation. Instead, they strangled the conversation by withholding nourishment. The poor sport just doesn't play well with others. She ignores the rules, pouts as it suits her, and quits the game without warning. At a cocktail party full of strangers, she is approached by a gentleman who introduces himself, and asks, *And what do you do?* Not wanting to play the small-talk game, she responds sarcastically with *In the event of what?* A lazy retort that has become common these days is

Back at you! For instance, *I love you, dear. Back at you!* This is right up there with the expression *Ditto!* as in *I truly enjoy spending quality time with you*, which garners the lackluster reply *Ditto*. This kind of noncommittal response cheats the person who first revealed their feelings.

Some poor sports simply have never been properly trained; they don't know how to ask open-ended questions themselves. With an outreach program, some of them show promise. You can help out a poor sport by answering a closed-ended question as if it had been open-ended. For instance, if a poor sport asks, *How was your weekend?* don't just say, *Great. What about yours?* Instead, teach by example. Offer, *Great. We took the kids skiing and it was a perfect day. The only glitch was that Mike took a bad spill, but he's okay now.* You have helped out the poor sport because you've given her lots of material with which she can ask a related question to keep the conversation from a reaching a quick demise. You've offered information about yourself that can help bridge distance and create conversation.

Playing the conversation game is an important ingredient to a successful conversation. How do people at work, on a date, or during a volunteer activity get to know you? Disclose a bit about yourself, if the receiver has the time and interest, and you will be making a contribution to keeping the conversation going. One-word answers are meant for the occasions when you are certain the inquiry is rhetorical or if you have a different agenda. Larry David dedicated a segment of his show *Curb Your Enthusiasm* to avoiding the "stop and chat." When you happen to run into someone you know on the street, at the grocery, walking down the hall, at back-to-school night, the decision over whether to wave and keep walking or stop and chat with them is usually an awkward one. Larry David has clarified that the "stop and chat" should only be reserved for true friends. I don't necessarily agree with Mr. David in all situations, however, as when you have the time to connect, every conversation can turn into an opportunity. Building rapport with fellow parents, workplace colleagues, volunteers, and neighbors during a five-minute "stop and chat" is a great investment of time. Lazy conversationalists are truly guilty of criminal negligence . . . too much effort to play the conversation game, so one-word answers are the norm. Autopilot responses such as "not much," "busy," or "good" do not keep the conversation going and can make for a miserable evening out, coffee date, or lengthy side-by-side walk to the conference room.

When you have the interest in and time for connecting, try offering a factoid about yourself:

Playing the Conversation Game

"How are you?" *"Fine."*

"What's new?" *"Same old, same old."*

"What has been going on?" *"Not much."*

Instead:

"How was your weekend?" *"Crazy with junior hockey car pools."*

"How's work?" *"Hectic, I spent a day attending an educational conference."*

"How's the project?" *"Bold new world for me, lots of new challenges."*

"What's new?" *"Working on my vegetable garden. I always start with high hopes."*

"How are you?" *"Great, looking forward to a visit from my brother next month."*

"How have you been?" *"I'm finding my footing in this new role at work."*

"How's school?" *"I am enjoying my speech class more than I expected."*

"How are things going?" *"Planning our annual meeting, which is hybrid this year."*

One cautionary note: It is very easy to become the monopolizer in the presence of a poor sport. Exercise restraint and keep tossing the ball back to the other person. Offer information that will contribute to the conversation, but don't steal the show! Until you are certain that there is time for further conversation, offer nothing more than a sentence when playing the conversation game. The bonus is that even if there is no interest shown, you have planted a seed about yourself. You are three-dimensional, you drive hockey car pool, you plant vegetables, you are planning the annual meeting.

THE KNOW-IT-ALL

These nasty criminals will mow you down with arrogance and condescension. They know everything, and they tell you so. They just knew that the stock market was going to take a dive or hit a high. In fact, they knew that the election would be close, that the winter was going to be brutal, et cetera. There is just no end to what they know about the sure-to-be Super Bowl win, how kids should be raised today, and why New Year's resolutions are a waste of time. Since they know that they are always right, they see no point in soliciting other opinions. They cut them down without compunction. In seconds they can silence an entire group because no one wants to risk humiliation at the hands of the know-it-all. Watch out for the person who has absolutely no interest in anyone's opinions but their own.

Be careful if you flaunt your opinions. Make sure others realize you are only offering your personal opinion about what works for you. *Conversation should be about building relationships, not winning fights.* Any time you talk with someone, you risk misrepresenting a fact, not recalling a news item correctly, disclosing personal bias, mistaking your facts, or saying something offensive. And your conversation companion risks the same. Thought leader Adam Grant states beautifully: "You are entitled to your own opinions in your head. But if you choose to express them out loud, it's your responsibility to:

1. Ground them in logic and facts
2. Explain your reasoning to others
3. Change them when better evidence appears."

There is one simple question, in two different forms, that, when used properly, prevents anyone from becoming a know-it-all. The two four-word queries are: *What is your opinion?* and *What are your thoughts?* Use either after stating an opinion or thought:

- "Home prices are definitely rising. What are your thoughts?"

- "Concussions are a huge problem for football players of all ages. What is your opinion?"

- "No way can you grow green beans in this climate. What do you think?"

THE ADVISER

The adviser always leaves her calling card at the scene of the crime. She is readily identifiable by her endless array of solutions to everyone else's problems. She's a veritable Ann Landers, Miss Manners, Oracle at Delphi, and Dr. Ruth rolled into one. There is nothing she can't solve— even when you don't want solutions! She generously offers unsolicited advice without charge.

Despite her generous nature, the adviser is a true outlaw. She decimates a perfectly good chat by meddling. The truth is, most people don't want advice—they want empathy, compassion, and simply to be heard. When the adviser rides in on her white horse to save the day, she minimizes the very person she's trying to rescue. She presumes that in hearing a tiny snippet of another's dilemma, she has an intimate understanding of the problem and knows the perfect solution. The adviser would do much better digging deeper to learn more about the issue and offering support instead of unsolicited solutions.

The adviser is very seductive because she is upbeat, confident, and wants to help. That's what makes her so wily. It is easy to unwittingly emulate her. In fact, I just did my impersonation of the adviser and was mortified once I realized it! I was having lunch with my friend Bill, who recently received a promotion to manager of a large sales territory for a medical supply company. He was talking about the difficulties with a new sales rep: the guy's sales were off, he wasn't making headway, he was discouraged, and so on. Well, I just chimed right in with all the solutions for him. I said, *I think the key to success is sell, sell, sell. Visibility is everything. I just kept knocking on doors till they started opening.*

Bill didn't need my advice; he needed my support. He just wanted to talk about his difficulties and share his thoughts. In giving solutions, I wasn't empathic. I was presumptuous. Bill did not ask for advice. He wasn't seeking my infinite wisdom—he wanted an attentive ear. Don't make the same mistake. Give the gift of listening and offer advice only when it's solicited.

Advisers are everywhere. I had an encounter with one on the ski slopes of Colorado. I was in Vail to teach a Small Talk seminar to ski instructors. I decided to ignore my fear of heights and take a ski lesson to better see how the instructors might best use small talk. I was grouped with a family from Alabama who had never even seen snow before. As the lesson progressed, the instructor noticed how cautiously I was skiing—I was even more reticent than the Alabamians! The instructor decided that I must have weak quad muscles. He showed me some strengthening exercises to solve that problem.

The real problem was that the adviser/instructor diagnosed the difficulty without even consulting me. He had no idea that I am an avid runner; my quad strength is fine, thank you very much! It was my terror at standing at an altitude of over eleven thousand feet that practically paralyzed me. Had the instructor bothered to find that out, he would have given me a much more effective skiing lesson. Had he dug deeper, he would have discovered that his premature analysis of my problem was completely incorrect.

Physicians are among the most notorious advisers. They frequently interrupt the patient and diagnose the problem before the patient has a chance to tell the whole story.

Frequently, the patient doesn't get to the heart of the matter until the doctor has his hand on the doorknob, about to exit the room. If the doctor would sit and listen to the patient completely before rendering an opinion, the appointment would be much more successful. Each would enjoy reduced frustration and a better outcome! The best way to avoid the doorknob problem is to ask: "Is there anything else I should know?" Whether you are selling, providing a service, negotiating, managing a difference of opinion with your spouse, or learning about your child's difficult day, this is the perfect prescription to learning the rest of the story.

Does the following conversation seem familiar?

Steve: How was your day?

Debra: I had a rough day.

Steve: What's going on?

Debra: I have a mound of paperwork to complete for a proposal, and I haven't packed for my trip to Seattle tomorrow. I am really behind.

Steve: Haven't I told you a million times, Deb? If you would just work smarter instead of harder. You should let your assistant prepare

the proposals, and why didn't you pack over
the weekend instead of waiting till the last
minute? You should plan better.

Debra: First of all, if it weren't for the last
minute, nothing would get done. Second
of all, when I start telling you how to
work on people's teeth, then you can start
telling me how to run my business!

I am picking on my husband. But I can be equally as
bad or even worse:

Debra: Good morning, Steve. How did you
sleep?

Steve: I had a terrible night. Couldn't get to sleep
for the longest time and then tossed and
turned.

Debra: Steve, why don't you try exercising or
reading a book to relax?

There I go offering unsolicited advice. All my husband
wanted was a response like:

Debra: Oh Steve, that must be so frustrating.

Acknowledge that what has been said is important. Providing unsolicited advice is not welcome in almost any situation.

A CRIME-FREE CONVERSATION

These eight criminals can bleed the life right out of any conversation. Sure, there are criminal lookalikes, too. Most of those folks are petty criminals specializing in misdemeanors that can hurt a good gab session but can't kill it. You have the skills to deal with these kinds of infractions. However, when you recognize one of the Most Wanted, exercise extreme caution. Even the most vigilant conversationalist can still get ambushed. You can even take down your own conversation, because the truth is, we each have a rap sheet. I'm a chronic interrupter when I don't police myself. Chances are that unless you are impersonating Mother Teresa, you have a conversational weakness that could land you on the Most Wanted list if you're not careful. Be on the lookout for your own criminal activity, for you may be aiding and abetting the murder of a good conversation.

Even if you take the high road and have a clean conversational record, you never know when you'll find yourself with a convicted felon on the loose slaughtering perfectly good small talk. Sometimes there's nothing that can be done except to preserve your own safety with a quick getaway. Knowing that, it behooves you to have several escape routes planned so you can exit in a hurry if need be. Fear not—I wouldn't leave you in harm's way. Your escape hatch is waiting.

10

FUMBLING THE CONVERSATION BALL

Navigating uncomfortable and awkward conversations requires dexterity. Preparation and sensitivity are the keys to avoiding these blunders and missteps.

TACKLE TOUGH CONVERSATIONS

Are there really any words to share with someone suffering from the loss of a loved one? We try to offer comforting words, but the majority of us mess up on what to say. How do we best talk to a friend, colleague, or family member who is in pain or enduring distress? Why is it so hard? Sometimes, because the person we are trying to comfort isn't ready to be comforted by words, and often because we choose the wrong words. Either way, this can lead to misinterpretation, frustration, and sometimes more hurt.

Our inclination is to help "fix" the person who is suffering. We attempt to apply logic to the situation rather than understanding that we need to look at the situation from a purely emotional state, just like the griever. Some words or phrases will be extremely painful for a grieving loved one to hear. Clichés and trite comments diminish loss or personal misfortune by providing simple answers to an extremely difficult reality. Comments like: "Time heals all wounds," "You still have so much to be thankful for," or "You must be relieved that she's out of pain" are not helpful and can even make grieving more difficult.

Don't Say . . .

He will get over it. (How would you know?)

You can try again.

She is in a better place.

There are no accidents.

It was just her time.

It could be worse, I know someone who . . .

You have years ahead of you to find love.

It will get easier.

You can always get another dog.

The best die young.

He lived a good, long life.

I know just how you feel. (You don't!)

You need to be strong now.

This too shall pass.

Business will bounce back. (How the heck do you know?)

Instead Try These Empathetic Statements:

You must feel as though the pain will never end.

You must really be sad; let me hug you again.

I would like to come by tomorrow and . . .

It isn't fair, is it?

I am available to visit with you.

Can I call you tomorrow?

Take all the time you need.

Tell me some special memories when you were a child . . .

My favorite memory of your loved one is . . .

I know what a beloved family member your dog was, my heart goes out to you.

You are not alone, I am here for you.

One of my dearest friends lost her son Andrew in his early thirties. I have found it so valuable to always keep him in mind whenever we talk:

- I'd love to hear stories about Andrew.

- I'm thinking of you. I know this is another Thanksgiving without Andrew.

- I'm keeping you and your family in my thoughts. I realize it cannot ever be the same without him.

- I know the holidays will be hard on you and your family without Andrew here with you.

- May I come visit with you during this holiday?

- I remember when Andrew . . .

One of my favorite pieces of advice on how to talk to someone grieving comes from the memoir *Becoming Duchess Goldblatt*: "If you've ever wondered what the right thing is to say to someone who is grieving a death, I think this is it: Tell me all about your dear one . . ."

Sadly, grief, loss, and misfortune are not under our control. The conversation territory we head into now is definitely filled with potholes but hopefully ones we can avoid.

> *It's hard to hate people up close. Move in.*
> —*Brené Brown*

Unless talking with likeminded folks, political, money, and religious conversations are fraught with social peril—which may explain why deep, connecting conversations do not occur; instead we choose the safe lane with sports and the weather. I know from experience and truly believe that small talk can lead to learning, change of perspective, and growth, so I am a fan of political dialogue. I wish we had more plain old small talk, especially between our government representatives. Talking of the "old days" rarely bears fruit, but I do long for the days when representatives even from opposing sides dined, golfed, and just hung out with each other. It is harder to be dismissive of another's views if you know their wife is enduring breast cancer treatments or her son is struggling in school. Without small talk to lubricate these harder conversations, we have lost the high touch and replaced it with divisiveness, bullying, and mean-spirited attacks. It's easy to do with strangers and acquaintances on social media platforms, as we have no personal connection to them.

TALKING POLITICS

Who are you voting for?

_____ will never win.

Are you a Democrat or Republican?

Do you have liberal or conservative views?

You are wasting your vote on _____.

These are all questions and statements filling our homes, social networks, and social and even business interactions. With elections more contentious than ever, political debates are likely infiltrating the office, dining tables, and social events, making it more important than ever to be wise about your political comments. Here are some tips to remember when entering into political conversations:

Consider establishing rules. Simply ask permission to set down some ground rules: "I don't want to debate you, but I do want permission to share and hear conflicting opinions," can help initiate and manage a political conversation. Also, be sure to offer a safe place for your conversation partner to do the same.

Show respect by offering, "Your thoughts and perspective are important to me, I want to hear from you and I don't assume I'm right."

Top Ten Tips for Political Conversation

1. Know your audience. If you engage in a political conversation with a business colleague, a friend, or social acquaintance, make sure you have an idea of their position. If you aren't sure, try asking a more open-ended question that may elicit a defining response: "What are your thoughts on the election?" Tailor your comments to be nonoffensive and not permanently damaging.

2. Know your stuff. Be prepared with accurate information about current political happenings so you project credibility.

3. Debate facts, not feelings. Keep emotionally driven statements out of your political discussion and stick to hard facts. This way, you don't hurt anyone's feelings and your own feelings don't get harmed. You will be less vulnerable in the end.

4. Respect! Respect yourself, your political candidates, your friends, family, and coworkers. Always be thoughtful of what you say and how you say it.

   - I can tell you're really frustrated by this issue.
   - You seem really excited about that event you attended.
   - I hear you're hopeful about _____.

5. Speak up or shut up. There's no harm in tastefully expressing your views, but don't feel pressured to share your thoughts. Just make a personal decision to talk or not talk about it up front and stick with it. Flip-flopping makes you a target for confrontation.

6. Listen to what is being said. A powerful political conversation has two sides. Take time to hear what your conversation partner says and appreciate their opinion. Ask questions you think will enhance the dialogue.

7. Know when to back down, turn around, and walk away. Think before you speak. If you feel like the conversation is getting too intense or uncomfortable, excuse yourself. Read body language to help keep your comments in check.

8. Agree to disagree. It's fun to have stimulating political banter, but if you agree to disagree up front it can be more entertaining and less destructive.

9. Remember you're on the same side. At the end of the day, you will probably continue to attend the same back-to-school nights, participate in the same social circle, and definitely remain in the

same family, so don't let political conversations interfere with your relationships.
10. If in the workplace, know the company's policies. Know what is and isn't allowed in the way of political expression (e.g., sending out political emails, hanging signs) and adhere to management requests.

Don't forget to approach difficult conversations differently when they're written as opposed to spoken. All form of written communications via email and posted on platforms are forever. All it takes is a screenshot of your tweet for your statement, right or wrong, to live in infamy.

And if you do fumble the ball, you can always slow things down. Political and religious views spark conversation firestorms fueled by verbal and written oxygen. Asking "What did you mean by that?" in a nonprovocative tone may help understanding. When involved in a heated argument that's headed nowhere, ask: "What proof would it take to change your mind?" If they can't give you an answer, stop wasting your time.

11

THE GRACEFUL EXIT

Whether you are trying to escape a convicted conversation killer or just want to circulate more, there are ways to artfully exit a conversation that leave the other person's ego intact. I find that many people remain in a conversation longer than they should for two reasons: they feel trapped, especially if it's just a two-person dialogue, or they are so comfortable that they don't want to leave. Comfort begets complacency. Why would I risk rejection with a stranger when I can stay here with you and talk sports? If you are at a party or an industry meeting and your goal is to meet people, you must find the courage to leave a conversation in order to accomplish your goals. Done properly, an authentic farewell will actually enhance your relationship.

When you prepare to depart a conversation, recall why you originally connected with your conversation partner and bring the conversation back to that topic. Doing so will allow you to make a meaningful connection and then take your leave easily. For instance, I was at an open house thrown by a large corporation. Before I left my conversation partner, I said, *Tom, it's been wonderful talking with you about the changes impacting the health-care industry. I need to catch up with another client before she leaves. Thanks for sharing your expertise.* Tom returned the compliment, we shook hands, and I headed to my client while Tom went in another direction.

Notice that I didn't make excuses for my leaving. I didn't say I had to call the babysitter or that I needed to return a text. That well-known adage "honesty is the best policy" is really true. It's important to retain your poise and state your reason for departing courteously. Even if you despised the conversation and are chomping at the bit to leave, be tactful as you go. Here are some diplomatic ways to make your exit:

Exit Lines

- I need to go see the exhibits.
- I want to go talk to the speaker.
- I'm going to circulate and meet some of the new members.
- I want to see if there are any other people from my industry here today.
- I must speak with the membership chairperson before she leaves.
- I promised myself that I'd meet three new people before I leave this evening.
- I want to meet some other potential clients this morning.
- I want to get around and say hello to everyone at this meeting/party.

These exit lines are successful because they put the focus directly on you. You clearly state that the reason you are leaving the conversation is that *you need to do something*. There is no mistaking the fact that you have a specific agenda that you are trying to accomplish. By highlighting your own goals, you take the burden off your conversation partner. Your small-talking associate now knows that your need to move on has nothing to do with the quality of time you just spent with that person. Or you can borrow the late actor George Plimpton's strategy for departure from bores at parties. Plimpton said he always carried two drinks. If he found himself talking to someone he wished to escape, he politely excused himself by saying he had to deliver the other drink.

The cardinal rule of the exit is that when you depart, you do what you said you were going to do. If you said good-bye to Joanne by telling her that you were going to see the exhibits, go do it. If you allow yourself to get sidetracked en route to your new destination, you run the risk of insulting your former partner. For instance, if Vince stops you on your way to the exhibits, do not stay and talk! Instead, say, *Vince, it's good to see you. I was just on my way to the exhibits. Would you like to join me or can I catch up with you afterward?* If you make the mistake of getting immersed in a conversation with Vince, all Joanne sees is that you didn't go to the exhibits. She now presumes that you were never headed there, and that your true goal was just to end the conversation. You now have a tarnished reputation, an upset person, and other possible unintended consequences. Don't burn a bridge by failing to get to your next destination!

TAKING CARE OF BUSINESS

Staying focused on your own agenda will make your small talking much more productive than if you are just casually mingling with whoever walks through the door. You will have questions prepared and a cast of characters in mind that you'd like to meet. Keeping track of your own progress toward accomplishing your objectives will help you gain the motivation to exit one conversation and get involved in another. It also provides you with a number of getaway lines.

You can invoke your partner's help in exiting by getting a referral or asking for business. For instance, you've been talking to Shelly for about fifteen minutes and you need to see some other people before the cocktail party ends. Shelly can actually help you do that if you let her. You say, *Shelly, I've been having trouble with the graphics package on my Apple at home. Do you know anyone here who uses this program??* Shelly will either give you a lead to the appropriate person, or she'll say she doesn't know anyone with that program. Either way, you've created a clean break. If Shelly can't help you, you simply thank her, tell her that you really need to find someone, and say goodbye. It's that easy. Don't invent a problem just to end a conversation.

Mentally check your agenda and ask for a referral to someone connected to forwarding your goals.

Suppose you want to find a prospective client or a new job for yourself. If you came to the party with that agenda, you need to verbalize it to accomplish it. You can do this easily without putting your conversation partner on the spot. You simply say, *Patrick, do you know anyone who might have some ideas about where I could find a human factors engineering opportunity?* A question such as this nets you a couple of good results. First, it lets the other party know in a very unobtrusive way that you are in the job market. Patrick just might be able to help you. The second accomplishment is that you've opened up channels with other people. Patrick may say, *I'm sorry I can't help you with that, Debra, but Jim, over there by the bar, is an engineer. He probably has some ideas for you.* You can graciously leave the conversation and head over toward someone who may be able to assist you with your goal. You easily introduce yourself to Jim, saying, *I was just talking with Patrick, and he told me that you're an engineer.* You have an introduction and a topic of conversation with no effort or angst. You may even get a new job out of the deal!

Don't hesitate to ask for business or referrals as you

take your leave from a conversation. Every person at a business meeting has an agenda—and virtually everyone there is seeking new talent or investment of some kind. There is no shortage of ways to ask for referrals or business. Here are some methods to take care of business; try some out and tailor a couple to fit your personality:

Business: Ask for Referrals

- Can you recommend anyone who needs a _____; I'd appreciate the referral.
- Can you suggest anyone with whom I could speak about _____?
- Who do you know that might be able to help me with _____?
- I had hoped to meet someone who is interested in _____. Do you know anyone like that?
- Who else here could I speak to about joining the _____ committee?

These techniques are not unique to business situations. You can easily adapt them to social events, as well. Here are some examples:

Social: Ask for Referrals

- I'd like to find someone who's interested in hiking or who has info on hiking groups. Do you know whether anyone here can help me?
- Do you know anyone here who's also new to this area?
- I'm going to look for someone interested in volunteer activities.
- Who do you know that might enjoy watching the New York Giants game this Monday night?
- Anyone you know that also has a second grader?
- Will you direct me to other new people to the neighborhood?
- Who do you know here that might know about a nanny share?
- Are there any other singles here that you can introduce me to?

THE CHANGING OF THE GUARD

A time-honored tradition of leaving a conversation is executing the changing of the guard. When a new person enters the group and begins talking to one or two people, one or more other people bow out. It is a quick and easy escape used by people all the time. The downside of this technique is that it *only* facilitates an exit, but if you are just looking for the nearest emergency exit, this is your ticket.

A slight variation on the theme is to take your conversation partner with you as you exit. This can be done even when it's just the two of you talking. You introduce your conversational party to someone who can render assistance to him. This transition is easily made with statements like these:

Ask Them to Join You

- I'd like to introduce you to an associate of mine who's in your field. Let's see if she's around.
- Matt is a great guy with an interesting history. I'd like to introduce you two.
- Let's go meet the speaker.
- I see my friend Jennifer is here. Let's go say hi.
- Let's circulate. I promised myself I'd meet some new people.
- Let's go get some dinner.

Issuing an invitation for your partner to join you on your way to another destination is a very gracious and considerate way to exit. You are still focused on your own agenda, but you haven't left your associate high and dry. Reverse the situation and think about the other person inviting you to join her. It's a perfect opportunity to get introduced to another person, or you can gracefully decline, feeling positive about the offer.

During the first few moments of a virtual meeting or a phone call, let the long-winded talker along with the no-regard-for-time colleague know in advance that you have a "hard stop," i.e., "I've got a hard stop at 1:55 in anticipation of another meeting at 2." Interrupting with a "gotta go" line is not going to win friends.

One last tip for exiting conversations: The white flag we used with the monopolizer is equally handy for gracefully leaving. The white flag indicates to our conversation partner that the conversation is almost over, there is about one lap left, same as car racing. Here are some white flags:

I've got about two minutes left before my hard stop, is there anything else I should know before signing off?

Need to take off in a couple minutes to pick up the kids, what else is happening for you?

My deadline for the buyer is later this afternoon. Before I head out, would you recommend that golf course?

I see a client just arrived. Before I head over there, what is the biggest challenge you are facing on this project?

Before I take off, tell me why you chose University of Maryland.

A LITTLE APPRECIATION GOES A LONG WAY

Ending a conversation by showing appreciation for the interchange provides an upbeat way to leave on a positive note. Thanking others for their time, expertise, or the sheer joy of the conversation is always welcome. You emanate poise and self-confidence when you bid adieu by expressing your gratitude and praising your partner in some way. This is accomplished in much the same way as using a compliment to forward a conversation, and the same rule applies: Be genuine. Done sincerely, offering gratitude will produce a wave of goodwill and a positive association with your name. Appreciation is a compliment with closure. You've ended the conversation on a personalized note, and both you and your partner separate feeling good about each other. Some ways to do this are shown here.

Show Appreciation

- It was wonderful to see you and hear about the convention.
- I've really enjoyed talking with you about your new business.
- I am glad you are enjoying your return to the office.
- I appreciate your willingness to share your expertise.
- Thank you for the delightful conversation.
- I'm so glad you introduced me to the subject of _____. It's very interesting.
- It's nice to meet someone involved in _____.
- It was so thoughtful of you to introduce me to _____. Thanks.
- I appreciate your effort to include me in the conversation. It's tough being new, and you made it easier for me.
- Your nephews sound like a handful.
- The lack of resources for this project is mind boggling.
- Your coursework for this program does seem overwhelming.
- Shaking my head at how impossible it can be to manage remote work and kids.
- Congratulations on creating a shop on Etsy.

Remember to end the conversation the same way you began it—with a smile and a handshake. Even if you have to get up and walk around the table to do this, make sure you do. You make a lasting impression when you seal a conversation with a handshake. Just that fleeting hand-to-hand moment enhances the rapport you've worked hard to establish. Melting away into the crowd discredits your integrity and your intentions. The end of the conversation represents the last opportunity to establish a connection with someone. Capitalize on it with a vengeance! If your interaction is virtual, say goodbye with names if at all possible. Especially if you are the leader: "Thanks for your input, Beatrice, Adrian, Gayle."

PARTING IS SUCH SWEET SORROW

If you've met someone with whom you'd like to further a relationship, the best way to exit is to ask to see him again. Assume the burden of issuing the invitation. If you are female, do not think that you have to wait for the male to extend the offer—whether it's a business or social engagement. If you are single and looking for ideas on how to issue invitations, please refer to Chapter 14, "Surviving the Singles Scene." This is about using small talk successfully to accomplish your goals. If your goal was to meet a new person and cultivate a relationship, then do so. Gender is immaterial.

Muster your moxie and just do it. Sure, you'll feel a bit out of your comfort zone, but the only way to pick the fruit is to get out on a limb. Realize that if you get turned down, it's not a statement about you—the other person doesn't know you well enough to draw any conclusions about you. Remember my friend Rex? His shyness was the reason he didn't invite me to sit with him. If someone turns you down, you can't possibly know the reason unless it is offered. Here are some ways to invite the other person to continue the relationship:

Issue an Invitation

- I don't want to monopolize your time this evening. Can we arrange to meet later?
- Will I see you at the next meeting?
- I'll be thinking of you during your _____. May I call you when you get back?
- I'd enjoy spending some time with you. Can I phone you to set up a convenient time?

- I'll email that article we discussed to your office next week. I'll phone you and schedule a time to see if we can find interest in working together. Will that work?
- I'd like to rehash what we did in class tonight. Would you like to join me for a cup of coffee?
- I enjoyed working out with you. Do you want to meet next week and do it again?
- I hope we can do business together soon. May I shoot you an email in the coming days to determine your level of interest?
- I'm glad to meet you and I would like to learn more about your organization. Will you welcome a phone call?

Before you leave a conversation, have a clear destination in mind. You don't necessarily need to head to another conversation. Feel free to get something to eat, get a fresh beverage, call the sitter and check on the kids, use the restroom, or even take a stroll around the room. Movement attracts attention, so make sure that you don't look lost. If your former conversation partner perceives that you're wandering around aimlessly, he's likely to feel insulted that you prefer your own company to his.

Because the manner in which you exit a conversation leaves a lasting impression, you want to develop finesse with graceful departures. There is nothing mysterious about these techniques, no rocket science required. They are commonsense tips, but they are not common practice. Practice frequently until you can comfortably disengage yourself from conversations using a variety of methods. Acquiring this skill will undoubtedly improve your overall confidence and presence. That enhanced poise will, in turn, make you an ever-more-inviting conversation partner.

12

THE CONVERSATIONAL BALL IS IN YOUR COURT!

Review the following cheat sheet full of dos and don'ts before any event, occasion, meeting, interview, or date. Keep it close by in a jacket pocket or a handbag, go to whatever meeting, luncheon, or party awaits, and seize the day!

Do be the first to say hello.

Do smile and appear approachable.

Do take the risk and introduce yourself to others.

Don't hope that your grandmother from St. Louis will arrive and introduce you to all these strangers.

Don't appear nervous or ill at ease; pretend you feel comfortable until you do!

Do extend your hand and shake hands with everyone you meet.

Do make eye contact.

Don't use nicknames without permission!

Don't avoid using someone's name because it is hard to pronounce.

Do practice pronouncing a unique and unusual name so that you say it properly.

Do make people feel special by using their names during conversation.

Do ask a person's name if you've forgotten it.

Don't avoid approaching someone because you have forgotten their name.

Don't ignore people at a table or standing on the sidelines; include them in introductions.

Do prepare icebreakers that show a genuine interest and are tailored to the occasion or situation.

Do play the conversation game, offering information about yourself and your activities so others can learn about you.

Don't monopolize by speaking for more than four to five minutes—throw the conversation ball back and forth.

Do practice an "elevator speech," offering a couple of interesting sentences about your work.

Don't brag about your success, promotion, or salary!

Don't wait for the awkward moment to come up with something to talk about.

Do show that you are listening by paraphrasing what you have heard back to the speaker.

Don't imagine that being silent makes one a good listener. Offer verbal cues to be a conversation contributor.

Do give the gift of repeating your name if you think the possibility exists that someone has forgotten it.

Do be conscious of your open and closed body language.

Do offer connections and assistance to others to strengthen the connection.

Don't offer help and not follow through.

Don't be a know-it-all.

Do use humor whenever possible to overcome uncomfortable moments.

Don't tell jokes unless you're a master joke teller.

Don't allow conversations to become similar to a batting cage . . . question after question.

Do stay on top of current events, including topics that may not interest you but are a source of interest for others.

Don't assume everyone is as well informed as you about sports, fashion, or politics.

Do get excited about other people's activities and interests.

Don't melt away from conversations.

Do issue invitations to continue relationships.

Do regularly stay in touch with those you meet.

Don't just reach out to someone when you need them for something.

Don't be judgmental; people hold different opinions, attitudes, and beliefs.

Do make the effort to interact with colleagues and friends.

Do keep track of what you learn about people so that you can use that information in future communications.

Do use open-ended questions such as, "Tell me about . . ." and "How did you come up with the idea?" to jump-start a conversation.

Don't use close-ended, ritualized questions, such as "How are you?" and "What's going on?" and expect an enthusiastic response.

Do come prepared to change topics if a conversation has lost steam or encounters a roadblock.

Do compliment others about their behavior, possessions, or appearance.

Don't hold people hostage with a long-winded story.

Do exhibit "host" behavior and include everyone in conversation.

Do include quiet people in the group whenever possible.

Remember, every conversation is an opportunity, but it is up to you to always take the risk and assume the burden.

13

MAKE THE MOST OF
NETWORKING EVENTS!

Learn how to make the most of meetings, interviews, and networking events and come across as composed and self-assured when entertaining clients at conventions, trade shows, and other work-related functions.

Do you dread receptions, banquets, and other business-related social events? Does attending another open house make you want to run inside your own and lock the door? You're not alone. Many of us are apprehensive about these situations, because most of us either hate entering rooms where we don't know anyone or hate spending time with people we don't know well. Keeping a conversation going during such occasions is an ordeal.

But for business professionals, these occasions represent

opportunities to develop business friendships and broaden our networks. Whether you realize it or not, networking happens all the time.

During an awkward social gathering, demanding sales

Networking??

presentation, or a tough interview, small talk can turn a challenging situation into a success. Small talk connects us, whether the setting is business or social.

Everyone learns the technical skills required for their jobs, but not everyone places importance on conversational skills. The ability to talk easily with anyone is a learned skill, not a personality trait. Acquiring it will help you develop rapport with people and leave a positive impression that lasts longer than an exchange of business cards.

Here are a few tips business professionals can use to improve their small-talk skills. With a little practice and use of these tips, you'll be conversing at the water cooler or before board meetings and in hospitality suites effortlessly.

TURN EVERY CONVERSATION INTO SUCCESSFUL BUSINESS NETWORKING

Steps:

1. **Introduce and initiate.** Go ahead and start with a hello! Even if you recognize or slightly know someone, re-introduce yourself. Act as if you're the host and introduce new arrivals to your conversation partner or partners.

Be aware of how he introduces himself (you may know him as Charles, but maybe he goes by Chuck), and use his preferred name throughout your interaction. This will help you remember it in the long run and also establish a personal connection. By taking ownership and initiating a conversation, you will feel more in control to drive the direction of the exchange.

2. **Use an icebreaker. Don't act like an FBI agent.** Questions like *What do you do?, Are you married?, Do you have children?*, and *Where are you from?* lead to dead-end conversations. A good icebreaker not only provides a way to meet new people, but also helps jump-start conversations. For example, using an icebreaker such as "Tell me about your organization" is unique, yet does not pin someone down into labeling themselves. Some other valuable icebreakers you might use are:

- "Bring me up to date on your latest project."
- "What do you find to be the most enjoyable aspect of your job?"
- "Tell me about your history with _____."

- "How did you come to find yourself in the health care field?"

3. **Express interest and make an effort.** You have to be *interested* if you want to be *interesting*. **Remember, people want to be with people who make them feel special,** not people who are "special." Take responsibility to help people you talk to feel as if they're the only person in the room.

    Part of your job as a conversee is to get the other person to talk. Listen to what your conversational partner is saying and ask relevant follow-up questions. Take cues from them and make a mental list of questions you can ask to get them to elaborate. If you're talking to Malcolm in the marketing department, ask him to describe what projects he has been working on. This is a great way to brainstorm future projects, find out about potential clients, and build a lasting business relationship. That being said, be sure not to ask so many questions that you come off as an interrogator. There should be a flow and balance during the conversation.

4. **Find common ground.** Whether you're chatting with a new coworker or a fellow association member, it's important to stay on a related topic. As long as you stay on a subject you are both familiar with—like your specific field or the day's event—you'll be able to communicate easily.

- Why are you in the setting you're in? (the mountains, the city, the suburbs?)
- Did you find today's seminar helpful?
- Wasn't the new mission statement this week interesting?

Avoid controversial topics like politics, religion, personal relationships, and family issues, and stick to what you both know is applicable. **Show an interest in your conversation partner's opinion, too.** You're not the only person who has opinions about funding the space program or what the future holds for bitcoin.

5. **Overcome awkward pauses.** It's up to you to keep the conversation going if there are some uncomfortable pauses. **Be prepared.** Spend a few

minutes before an anticipated event preparing to talk easily about two to three topics. They will come in handy when you find yourself in the middle of an awkward moment . . . or while seated at a table of eight where everyone is playing with their food.

Say, "It's great having our sales conference in a warm, tropical place. Have you been to Marco Island before?" Use pauses as an opportunity to compliment your counterpart. Try, "I'm impressed with what you're doing for our business. You've made some huge improvements in our technology department over there." This is also a great time to interject with any material you've previously prepared. Listen carefully for information that can keep the conversation going.

6. **Stop conversation monopolists in their tracks.** If possible, wait for the person to take a breath or to pause, then break in with a comment about their topic. Immediately redirect the conversation in the direction you wish it to go.

7. **Join the conversation ready to play the conversation game.** When someone asks *How's business?* or *What's going on?* answer with more than

Not much. Tell more about yourself so that others can learn more about you. When waiting for a meeting to begin, your client asks how your summer is going. The lazy response is "Pretty good." Give a one sentence answer of substance instead: "Looking forward to some Nebraska walleye fishing." When asked how your day is going upon arrival for the Zoom meeting: "My day got off to a good start thanks to quick walk with my dog" or "Busier than usual because we have an educational conference tomorrow." You have supplied information about yourself that can be leapfrogged from if interest and time allows.

Be careful with business acquaintances. You wouldn't want to open a conversation with: *How's your job at_____?* What if that person just got fired or laid off? Be careful when you're asking about an acquaintance's spouse or special friend; you could regret it.

8. **Establish personal boundaries.** It's fine if you want to let someone know where you went to college or how many children you have, but be mindful of how much personal information you provide. Sure, your

relationship could benefit if you find out both your wives are attorneys, but evaluate the value of the subject matter and its impact on the rapport. If the dialogue gets too sidetracked into personal details, the business-networking angle can become lost. Revealing too many personal details in a business setting can be inappropriate. Use your best judgment to maximize the content of the conversation.

9. **Be aware of body language.** Nervous or ill-at-ease people make others uncomfortable. Act confident and comfortable, even when you're not.

10. **Exit thoughtfully.** In many business situations, it's important to make contact with several people and move around a room. Moving on makes sense sometimes. Don't melt from conversations. Find an appropriate point in the conversation to make an exit. Say, "I really enjoyed talking to you about today's program. I have your card and I'll be in touch with you this week so we can discuss it further." Or reach out via the chat box expressing your appreciation for their comments or questions. Let them know you want to stay in touch and will

issue an invite via LinkedIn. Make a plan that is actionable and give a specific time when you'll follow up. Most importantly, if you say you're going to do something, do it!

While much of this advice applies to direct communication, do not take networking techniques for granted on social media, especially LinkedIn. A missed opportunity is issuing a LinkedIn invitation without framing with a bit of small talk. Anything that is genuine:

"I admire your work and want to connect."

"Issuing this invitation because we attended the same webinar on investing."

"As an alum of Northwestern I would like to connect."

"We don't know each other; however, I saw a reference to your research and would like to connect."

Upon accepting the invitation add an acknowledgment:

"Glad to be connected"

"Thanks for reaching out."

"I appreciate your interest in connecting."

"Looking forward to finding mutual work interests."

Every encounter involves risk. As long as you keep looking for new people to meet, expand community and networks, and you show an interest in other people, you can make building relationships and networking meaningful and enjoy lively conversations.

14

SURVIVING THE SINGLES SCENE

Y ou enter a roomful of people. All of them seem to be happily engaged in conversation with someone else. You start to worry that others are going to judge you and find you lacking. You steel yourself for rejection. You almost turn and decide it's not worth it to attend this event.

You may be suffering from "social anxiety disorder." But chances are you're just attending a singles event and feeling the natural anxiety of putting yourself out there and making yourself vulnerable.

Probably the scariest social scene is one in which you are there specifically to meet other people. You don't have the purpose of networking to prop you up. You are simply there to connect with others. And for some strange reason in our society, that takes courage to admit.

Most of my single friends admit to me that they hate the dating scene. My sister Elisabeth, a biotech educator, says, *Dating? What's that? My single fortyish friends and I have all decided we're far too busy to date!*

But one friend, Suzanne, has been divorced for eight years and has little desire to change her circumstances. She'd be ecstatic to find the perfect man, but she refuses to settle for someone who's not right for her. She'd rather stay single and continue to play the field. To her, it's actually fun!

There are so many different situations that call for small talk in the singles scene that it's difficult to give one-size-fits-all advice. Are you in your twenties or your fifties? Do you prefer going to a bar, using a dating app, or attending an organized event? Are you a man or a woman, queer, gender-fluid, the indoor or outdoor type? But one piece of advice will cover all situations: Don't think of what you're doing as "singles" socializing. Just think of it as networking, building a community of likeminded people. You have something to offer others, and they have something to offer you: connection to humanity. And never forget, each and every person you connect with may introduce you to your "person."

PULL YOURSELF TOGETHER!

One of the most daunting aspects of singles socializing is making your entrance—actually walking in to where the action is taking place or arriving for your first face-to-face after twenty-two days chatting on Tinder. Even after a few video chats, the face-to-face date may feel overwhelming. It's important to understand that you don't have to make small talk immediately upon entering. Suzanne says she always takes a deep breath before she enters the room and visualizes pulling all her energy into her core, so that she's not sending out any "feelers" when she makes her entrance. She's literally pulling herself together!

If you are attending an event, stand in the doorway and survey the scene. This accomplishes two things: You get a moment to stabilize yourself *and* get your bearings, and you are framing yourself for everyone to see; they will perceive you as a self-confident person and unconsciously hope for the chance to speak with you. Self-confidence is probably the single most powerful magnet, right after good looks.

But after you walk into the room, pretend you're invisible. No one sees you, so you have no need to feel uncomfortable or insecure. Everyone else in the room is either too occupied with their own activity or conversation or else completely absorbed in their own feelings of uncertainty. You can wander around the room looking for food or drink and simply adapt yourself to the environment. Now is a good time to soak up the scene: Who's here? How does the crowd feel? Are people having a good time or is there a lot of tension? Look around. Who seems approachable?

As you make your observations, your thoughts will turn into words, which you can then share as you approach others or they approach you. It's always easiest to break the ice with a few observations about the situation, rather than asking for personal information. Normally, if you make an innocuous observation, the person on the other end will respond with their impressions. It's valuable to start small talking with a person that you are not necessarily attracted to; it is less intimidating and will get you over your stage fright. Plus, you never know, they might introduce you to someone *really* interesting!

Icebreakers for Singles

- I've been here before, but it's never been so crowded.
- Which way to the food (bar)?

- I know exactly zero people here. How about you?
- This food looks like it's pretty tasty.
- It looks like there are a lot of interesting people here. Do you know any of them?
- Would you please hand me a napkin?
- Friday afternoons are a great time for this kind of thing. Something to look forward to at the end of the week.
- I never know what to say, but I would like to meet you.

You know that "So, what do you do?" and "Where are you from?" aren't exactly the most scintillating questions to ask on a date—nor do they actually give you any juicy information about the person sitting across from you. If you *really* want to know whether you have good chemistry and long-term potential here, you need to probe deeper than that. Especially if you have covered the basic information via your dating app interactions. But what kind of questions do you ask? Don't worry, there are no right or wrong answers. You're judging whether someone shares your values and goals to see whether they'd be a good long-term partner. Or at minimum, a second date. And if not—if their answers are so wacky and opposite of what you believe that you don't think you'll last through the next fifty minutes, never mind the next fifty years—then at least you've had an evening of interesting conversation!

Here are some questions you can ask on a dating app, on the phone, or in person:

Question #1: "If your company gave one-year paid sabbaticals, what would you do for that year?"

Maybe he'd run off to a remote island in the Pacific or start his own business. Maybe she'd spend her days working in a soup kitchen. Whatever your date answers, this is a very revealing question, and a perfect one to ask on a first date. It reveals your date's true passions and priorities, showing you whether they are selfless, selfish, or overly ambitious. You'll also learn what this person cares about, but isn't making time for right now. Follow up with, "Are you doing anything like that right now?" Obviously she can't spend every day in the soup kitchen, but does she volunteer on weekends? And who knows—maybe you'll wind up bonding over your secret desire to play piano or start your own bike tour company.

Question #2: "What's the biggest misperception people
have about you?"

Maybe your date will say that everyone thinks he's snobby
and stuck-up, when he's really just shy. It's a good
thing to know—especially if you've been sitting across
from him thinking just that. You'll get a sense of how
the person views him or herself. And it gives you the
chance to take a step back and rethink your opinion of
them. This is a great first-date question, particularly if
you make the disclosure first. Say, for example, "Sometimes people think I talk too much, but I just tend to
babble when nervous. Is there anything you do that
you think gives people an off-base first impression of
you?" This gives you the opportunity to clear up any
misperceptions your date might have about you, while
also helping you know your "real" date without having
to pry.

Question #3: "What's the one life experience you want a
do-over on?"

Here's your chance to learn a juicy tidbit about your date's
past: Does she secretly wish she went to culinary school
instead of law school? Does he rue the day he gave up
his pet cat to clinch that great "no pets" apartment?

Everyone's got some regrets, and they speak tons about someone's character. Not sure how to segue into this heavy question? You're best off warming them up first with your own disclosure, whether that's how you wished you'd taken a year off after college just to travel or quit a bad job before it became a really, really bad job. Just say, "I'm pretty happy with how things are going right now, but the one thing I always wished I'd done differently is _____. How about you?"

Question #4: "Will you share an embarrassing moment with me?"

Is she secure enough to laugh at the time she gave a huge work presentation wearing her cycling shoes because she forgot to pack her work shoes? Can he share the embarrassment of falling off the chairlift his first time on a snowboard while trying to impress an ex? It's not the actual activity that matters—you want to know whether your date can be vulnerable around you early on. If someone's willing to share their private fiascos, you need to be ready to share some of your most embarrassing moments as well. In fact, it's probably best if you spill the beans first, and one easy way to do that is to say, "First dates make me kind of nervous, but I always remind myself it pales in comparison to the time, unbeknownst to me, I wore ketchup on my shirt during my first sales call!"

Question #5: "If your house were on fire, what's the one thing you'd make sure to save?"

Want to learn whether your date is sentimental or practical? Find out whether he'd rescue his grandfather's signed Hank Aaron ball or his Apple Watch. This question gives you a sense of what's valuable to someone and whether your values coincide. Make sure to ask why they'd grab that particular item—you may find she'd grab her college diaries because those were amazing years when she learned (and recorded) so much about life, or that he'd grab his vinyl record collection since his parents collected as well. And if you're wondering how you bring up such an odd topic, consider an opener like, "I have a lot of interests and hobbies, but what's truly close to my heart is fishing. In fact, my tackle box is the first thing I'd grab if my house were burning down. That, and of course my cat. How about you?"

FIND THE CONNECTION

While Suzanne says she loves playing the field, most people hope to find that special person with whom they can honestly connect. Think about the words *connection* and *relationship.* To "connect" or "relate" means to find commonality with another human being. You can begin looking for these connections as soon as you engage a stranger in small talk by offering something about yourself and by asking questions of the other person. Keep in mind that when someone responds to your comment or answers your question, they usually give you more fodder for small talk.

Connectors

- You look totally at ease. I wish I could feel the same way you do.
- That's a great outfit (pair of shoes, bracelet, necktie). I love fashion (good taste, jewelry).
- I almost stayed home to read a book instead of coming here.
- I love watching basketball, but this is fun, too.

- I've never attended one of these events before. What's your experience with this organization?
- How did you hear about this event?
- This is an interesting organization. Have you tried any of their outdoor events, like hiking or bicycling?
- It is so fun to finally meet up in person, do your text conversations typically go on as long as ours have?

FOLLOW UP ON THE CONNECTION

Consider the following approach when you ask a question or a question is asked of you. Think about how you will comment on whatever is said by your conversation partner. Here's an example:

You: How often do you go out?

Her: Almost every night.

As she's responding, think about how to comment on what she's saying, rather than on your next question. This exercise does wonders to sharpen your listening skills.

You: Now that sounds like a lot of work!

Comment on her response rather than asking a predictable follow-up question like *Where do you like to go?* It takes a higher level of listening to make a follow-up comment than it does to ask a follow-up question. If you had a follow-up question in mind that you were tempted to use but did not, then you are on the right path. Although you didn't follow with a question, it doesn't mean you shouldn't have had one at the ready. As a general rule, always formulate at least one follow-up question and keep it in your head even if you may not use it.

Instead of a witty or humorous follow-up comment, another option is to follow up with a disclosure. Let's see how this works:

You: How often do you go out?

Her: Almost every night.

You: Really? I used to be able to do that!

This time, a statement of self-disclosure rather than a comment keeps the connection going.

It's also helpful to have relevant follow-up questions in mind. Most of the time follow-up comments and disclosures will act as "prompters." They'll usually prompt the other person to speak or to ask you questions. Let's revisit the example:

You: How often do you go out?

Her: Almost every night.

You: Now that sounds like a lot of work!

(In this case the follow-up comment will act as a prompter.)

Her (laughing): Yeah, I know, it's like a full-time job!

When you comment on someone's response, they will be prompted to say something in return. Use it as connecting fuel.

What do you do when there is not a response to the follow-up comment or disclosure? Use one of the follow-up questions that you formulated and patiently kept around in your head. Let's go back to the example we've been working with:

You: How often do you go out?

Her: Almost every night.

You: Now that sounds like a lot of work!

Her: (laughs but no response)

You: Where do you like to go?

Here was a follow-up question that was relevant to the original question (*How often do you go out?*) and her response to it (*Almost every night*). Other potential questions could have been, *Where do you get all that energy?* or *How do you make so much time?*

Once you get into the habit of making follow-up comments and disclosures, adding in follow-up questions is a cinch. With creative use of these three elements (questions, follow-up comments, follow-up questions), the possibilities and variations in conversation are virtually limitless. As long as you stay focused on the conversation, you can keep it going.

ASKING FOR THAT DATE

Now that you have successfully small talked your way through the singles scene, you have a range of potential date mates. But actually asking for a date—putting your ego on the line and risking rejection—moves you to a whole different level. While Suzanne never calls a man for a date, Linda is adamant: "Why shouldn't I be able to choose whom I'd like to go out with? Just because I'm a woman doesn't mean I should just wait for some random person to choose me." She makes sure she's ready with the small talk whenever she phones a man for a date: "First I reconnect how we met. I refresh his memory about a couple of incidents at the event. I tell him how much I enjoyed our conversation there and mention that it would be fun to resume it over coffee or lunch. As assertive as I am, I never ask a man out for dinner on the first date. It seems less threatening—both to me and to him—to suggest something more casual."

My friend Bob offers this advice: "Have some date ideas in mind before you pick up the phone. I will call a woman and say something like, 'There's a wine tasting at Hudson Gardens on Thursday night. I was thinking we could go to that early in the evening and then maybe take a walk along the river. Or we could get some dinner somewhere near the gardens.'" Note that he doesn't call the person he's interested in and say *What are you doing Saturday night?*, which would offer her the perfect opportunity to answer, *Washing my hair.* Invitations like *Would you like to get together sometime?* are too vague. Be specific in order to receive a direct answer.

Bob's approach is to offer his potential date something specific for them to do together and, by the way, something that sounds like fun. At least for the first few dates, try to think of ideas that would appeal to your date rather than choosing something you'd like to do. Don't think that just because you like to go to the races, she will, too. The best dating advice I've heard is from a man who never asks for a date the first time he calls, texts, or emails. He exercises patience and waits until the second or third contact. Even then, he tries to suggest something that he might do with any friend, like a bike ride, a walk, or a gallery tour. This approach takes a little longer, but it builds real trust and affection before moving on to the heavier stuff. In the long run, he probably gets further faster and with a more satisfying outcome. Another piece of advice offered by my adult son that makes sense: Don't plan a movie/theater date for the first few dates. Interaction is key to getting to know each other.

Try to empathize with the person who's doing the calling. Courage is required of anyone asking for a date. When asked: *Friday or Saturday night?* or *What are you up for—a movie or some dancing?* please do not answer with: *Whatever.* A *Whatever* response indicates one of two things, neither one of them positive: You either don't care about this person or the conversation, or you don't know what you want. A cheerful comeback: *Saturday night sounds great* or *I'd be happy to go dancing with you either night* is appropriate.

ON THE DATE

People like to feel good about themselves. Dating is the perfect opportunity to do that for someone else. Make them feel like they're attractive and interesting. Focus on your date rather than worrying about what he or she is thinking of you.

My friend Janie emailed me this story: "I asked my date questions for two straight hours (he was very self-absorbed and asked zilch about me). And then there was silence, so I said to him: 'Okay, now you ask *me* some questions.' He thought a minute and then said, 'So how am I doing?' Definitely not a keeper."

Another friend tells the story about a guy she dated who was intensely connected with her as long as he was doing the talking. But as soon as she took her turn, his eyes would wander all around the room. She had listened politely and actively, and now he was sending her the message that she was boring him. She watched it happen for the last time when they went to dinner at an outdoor café. He was able to ignore all the beautiful women walking past—as long as he was doing the talking. But when her turn came, he would look beyond her, over her, anywhere but *at* her, in order to glimpse some attractive woman. My friend was hurt and offended. She got up and left, telling him, "You don't need me here. You can just talk to yourself and keep company with all the beautiful women walking by."

Initiating-the-Date Small Talk

- It was great to meet you at _____. I hope you had as good a time as I did.
- Hey, I wanted to add something to our text conversation the other night . . .
- You mentioned _____. Do you have any idea where I can find one?
- I really enjoyed our conversation about _____, and felt like we kind of connected on that issue/ topic. Would you like to go for coffee this weekend so we can continue the discussion?
- You mentioned to me that you like contemporary art. The art museum has a _____ exhibition until next month. Would sometime in the evening this week work for you?

- I remember you said that you were a fan of _____. I enjoy him, too. Do you want to go see his latest film sometime over the weekend?
- Your profile noted that cooking was a passion. How about a cooking class together at _____?

We all have stories we like to share, but of course since they're ours, we've heard them all before. So dating is a great opportunity to hear someone *else's* stories. Listen to them actively and empathetically—and even share some of your own when it's appropriate—but don't kill the conversation with domination. Listening is a great way to find out if there's something worth pursuing in that person sitting across from you.

Just a couple more words of advice: Be patient. You don't have to have it all in one date. Give yourself a chance to bond with this person instead of trying to find out everything about them in this one encounter and then making a snap decision about whether or not you want to see them again. And keep your sense of humor. Don't tell jokes (unless you're great at it), but allow yourself to be funny. As the late Larry King said, "Never stay too serious too long."

DATING WISDOM

Over the years, many of my readers and workshop attendees have shared their stories with me. Allow me to pass some of them on to you.

Leave your cell phone in the car. Paul gave up on dating but not before he had this experience to relate: "I was meeting someone for the first time after corresponding through email. It was an awful conversation anyway, but then her cell phone rang. Without so much as an 'excuse me,' she answered it. I promptly got up and left. Perhaps an overreaction, but it did get me out of there. So if you're giving advice, 'Turn off your cell phone' works for me."

My friend Mark was beyond frustrated with cell phone use during dating. If a date had his phone out or, worse, checked it, Mark's attack was stinging: "Unless you are in organ procurement I cannot imagine why you need to have your phone handy." What a great line! One that he never needed with his now husband, Joseph.

First Date Small Talk

- It's great to see you again. I'm so glad you were able to _____ with me tonight. Tell me about your day.

- So tell me a little bit about yourself: Who was your best friend growing up, how do you celebrate your favorite holiday, what do you eat for lunch?
- Did you go away to college?
- Where does your family live?
- I have two brothers and a sister. How about you, tell me about your family?
- What brought you to this city?
- Do you have any pets? Hobbies? Favorite activities during this season of the year?
- How do you like to spend your free time?

Careful what you say. This admonition comes from Patty, who shares this story: "My boyfriend, Rob, went out on a double date (prior to meeting me, of course) that was arranged with one of the partners at his office. His blind date was a friend of the partner's wife, and they were trying to set Rob up with her. On the date, the four of them watched a young lady walk by. She had a large, visible tattoo. Rob commented to his three tablemates, 'I don't understand why any young woman would get a tattoo. Don't they know that it's a huge turnoff?' Sure enough, his date, who was lovely in every way, had a tattoo."

Save your demands for later in the relationship.
Jim reveals his frustration in the telling of this tale: "A 'friend' fixed me up, a term I have learned to loathe, with a psychologist from Manhattan who specializes in working with sexually abused women and children. I (foolishly) said yes. I met Sarah at a wonderful restaurant in San Francisco. After we sat down, her first question was 'Have you had an AIDS test?' (I was immediately reminded of a woman friend who suggested, at the time of my divorce, that I have an AIDS test, which would make me more 'market-able.') I always try to find humor in a moment of adversity, so I suggested to Sarah that we order a drink first, then I'd fill out the questionnaire. Sarah was not amused. 'Look,' she insisted, 'it's the twenty-first century, and I'm not going to fool around with some guy who doesn't know where it's been!' Things went downhill from there. I went into my 'I'll seem smart by shutting up' mode and just listened for an hour to reports of spousal abuse, lover abuse, child abuse, shrink abuse, deadbeat everything. I shook Sarah's hand as we left the restaurant and said, 'Ahhhh, errrr, it's been . . . unique.' Amazingly, Sarah called me the next day and told me what a wonderful time she had—and . . . could we see each other again?"

"She was interested . . . but he was chicken . . ."

**Try some sensitivity before you blurt out opin-
ions.** My sister Terri, the political science professor, shared
this story, complete with a getaway technique. "I once had
a date with a guy who was very opinionated. He assumed,
though he never asked, that I felt just as he did about politics, religion, et cetera. So he went on at length on his Rush
Limbaugh tangent, insulting everyone on the opposite side
of each issue (me included) until finally he asked what I
thought. I said, 'I disagree with every single opinion you've
expressed.' How's that for an exit line?"

THRIVING IN THE SINGLES SCENE

Feeling comfortable and confident in conversation is the best way to not only survive but to thrive being single. Knowing how to "chat" helps you to make new friends and enrich old friendships. Practice helps, so put yourself out there where you're forced to small talk with other singles. Like everything else you do, the more you practice, the easier it becomes. And once you're good at it, it's even fun. Don't be afraid of looking dumb or saying the wrong thing. Laughing at yourself is the best way to develop a sense of humor (if you don't already have one) and, at the same time, make people feel less threatened by you. Every conversation is an opportunity to connect. We dismiss people because they are not our type or don't participate in certain activities or are not the gender we are attracted to. Observing friends and family in the dating pool in recent years, I see the stark differences and unique benefits of different kinds of apps. Some, like Tinder, offer the ability to "meet" as many as your sore swiping thumb allows. Hundreds of matches and nonmatches as rapidly as your thumb can scroll. This very fast-paced, unending resource allows for a quick "look." But others apps allow few matches, some only matching you with one person each day. This requires more patience and thoughtfulness and exploration beyond the posted pictures. And although appearance is an ingredient, there is lots more to ponder before moving forward to reach out to someone on these more selective apps, with pluses and minuses to both approaches. When using any dating app, remember to be intentional about your goals, whether it's just to meet people or make a real, lasting connection.

It was my wonderful friend Karen Thomas who announced at our book club meeting thirty years ago that she had someone in mind for me to meet. And thanks to her thoughtfulness and generosity of spirit, I was introduced to her periodontist, now my husband, Steve. Ask to be fixed up. Don't hesitate to ask friends to keep you in mind. And never dismiss someone because they are not your type. This person could become your friend and introduce you to your future partner.

15

THE FEEL-GOOD FACTOR

People part with their money for two reasons: to solve a problem and to attain good feelings. Look at it this way: It's hard to quickly evaluate the expertise of a new dentist, but you immediately know which one makes you feel more comfortable. You can take lessons from a highly qualified ski instructor, but if his silence makes you feel awkward while riding the chairlift together, you'll switch instructors. When Walmart and Target carry the same items at about the same prices and they're located close together, where do you buy? You choose the store where the returns are simpler, the people are friendlier, and the appearance is cleaner— where you are made to feel more welcome.

The feel-good factor underlies every aspect of life. Even

in the area of parent-teacher conferences, if your child's teacher delivers negative feedback in a way that shows empathy, not harshness, you're more likely to support the next vote to increase taxes that go toward schools. Similarly, in the corporate world, if you want a promotion but come across as aloof or reserved, you'll be overlooked in favor of someone who has warm "people skills"—skills that make others feel good about being around them.

Here's how to build rapport that leads to success in every business relationship.

- **Use small talk as a picture frame around business conversations.** Begin and end with small talk when making a presentation to a client, selling a widget, negotiating a contract, providing a service, or conferencing with your child's teacher. A study conducted with physicians showed those who spend a few minutes asking patients about their family, their work, or summer plans before and/or after an examination are less likely to be sued than those who don't. Let's face it. People don't sue people they care about. And we care about people who show they care about us.

- **Express empathy.** Everyone is entitled to be listened to, even when in the wrong. Consider the client who sees the stock market rise 30 percent but not his own portfolio. The stockbroker knows the client insisted on picking the stocks himself, but it would be a mistake to make the client "wrong." It's better to say, *I realize it's frustrating to experience this. What can we do from here?* That goes a long way to defusing negative emotions and helping the client feel better about this relationship—rather than tempted to move on to another stockbroker.

- **Greet people warmly, make eye contact, and smile.** Be the first to say hello. Be careful, you might be viewed as a snob if you are not the first to say hello. People often go back to their favorite restaurants because the host greets them with a sincere smile, looks at them directly, and welcomes them with warmth. My husband and I go to our favorite restaurant—and bring our friends there, too—because the wait staff, the host/hostess, and even the owner take the time to make us feel extra special.

- **Use the person's name in conversation.** You are more likely to get special treatment by using the person's name. When you call to clarify a credit card billing, for example, say: *Joe, thanks for taking the time to help me with this question.* That makes Joe feel his role is important. If you don't know someone's name, take a moment to ask, and then repeat it. Be sure to pronounce it correctly. And never presume your conversation partner has a nickname. My name is Debra, not Debbie. I don't feel good when people call me Debbie. It's a little thing that has big importance.

- **Show an interest in others.** In response to our high-tech environment of email and texting, we need "high touch" more than ever. That's what you create when you show an interest in the lives of your customers/clients/patients/members every chance you get.

- **Dig deeper.** When you engage in a conversation, don't leave it too quickly. If your customer/client/ patient mentions her vacation, pick up on the cue and dig deeper. Ask where she went, what she did, what the highlight was, if she would go back.

You'll make her feel good about her life and about taking time with you. Always follow up a question like *How's work?* with *What's been going on at work since the last time we spoke?* This way he or she knows you really want to hear about what is going on with work.

- **Be a good listener.** That means making eye contact and responding with verbal cues to show you hear what the speaker says. Verbal cues include the phrases: *Tell me more, What happened first?, What happened next?, That must have been difficult*, and so on. Using them makes people feel actively listened to.

- **Stop being an adviser.** When you mention a problem you might be having with an employee or an associate, do people offer advice without asking any questions? Have you ever put together a résumé and, as soon as you sent it out, someone told you it was too long or too short or too detailed or not detailed enough? Jumping in with unsolicited advice happens annoyingly often. Instead of advice, give understanding with simple phrases like

I know you can work out a solution or *I hope the job hunt goes well for you.* Offer advice only when you are specifically asked for it.

An example I use in my presentations really makes my point about the feel-good factor. I wanted to find a good print shop near my home and walked into one near the busiest post office in our state. I was greeted with a sign that read: LACK OF PREPARATION ON YOUR PART DOES NOT CONSTITUTE AN EMERGENCY ON MY PART. I thought, How many people would zip into this shop for a few photocopies before mailing off an important package? I doubt they would feel welcome here.

I then visited a print shop across the street. Two colorful signs posted there made my day. One featured a cactus and said, STUCK? WE'LL HELP YOU OUT OF A PRICKLY SITUATION. The other, showing a pot of jam, read: IN A JAM? WE'LL HELP YOU OUT OF A STICKY SITUATION. You can guess which printer made me feel better about forming a business relationship.

It's easy to start off on the wrong foot if you're not paying attention. "How are you?" Has this once-generic greeting become a conversation game changer in recent years? The once rhetorical and sometimes disingenuous greeting "How are you?" as well as "How have you been?" have taken on new meaning in an age of pandemics, climate change, school shootings, wars, and global upheaval. Faced with physical and social distancing, along with limited travel as well as economic challenges for many, staying in touch and cultivating connections with family, friends, professional networks and the community at large became a lifeline to the future. And these difficult times seemingly forever changed our landscape for conversation.

Have you thought about establishing forums or groups that can meet regularly to brainstorm or simply stay in touch? Our new lingo now includes "Zoom fatigue"; it's a challenge in virtual meetings to focus on or truly connect with others. How about some tips and tools to enhance your efforts?

Video calls, virtual gatherings, a phone call, or any type of meeting focused on business will benefit—now more than ever—from what I label "the picture frame of small talk" around each and every business conversation. So for a few minutes before and a few minutes at the end of the business meeting, lead and end with small talk. Carving out time at the start of meetings to catch up a little is a key ingredient. These connecting conversations create and enhance business friendships. Many meetings might start with some informal small talk, with coworkers sharing small pieces of their lives and families. This is a good thing: Research shows that team members who share personal information perform better than teams that don't. When leaders model this, it often boosts team performance even more. But the switch to video conferencing can sometimes make it feel like you have to get down to business faster.

Meanwhile, staying in touch with family and friends frequently becomes patterned, leading down the path to rhetorical conversations. For a nonbusiness call, how about a one-minute check-in per participant to launch each get-together? Ask each person to contribute one minute on:

Their favorite WFH (work from home) outfit

Best use of time thanks to elimination of commute

Bucket list for rest of the year or the year ahead

Book, movie, TV, or podcast recommendation

For any type of virtual get-together, social or professional, request participants to be prepared to display a picture from their past week or month during the first few minutes. This is fun and gives each participant a window into each other's real life.

During our face-to-face conversations, we pick up on social and visual cues: someone leaning forward who might wish to add to the conversation, or someone with a bewildered expression responding to a point that is made. But these cues can be harder to see on video, potentially resulting in people speaking up less, talking over each other, or simply a lack of connectivity in the conversation.

Visual listening cues can make a difference. For example, when you need to engage, keep your eyes focused on your fellow video chat participants, instead of on your inbox, social media, or your own beauty, and show that you're listening by nodding and smiling. This will help everyone better read emotions, stay on top of the conversation, and maintain a link to the conversation.

And you don't have to be restricted to scheduled meetings for small talk. Setting aside time for informal video chatting with coworkers, friends, and family over coffee or lunch breaks to build connections and boost morale is an important ingredient to building rapport. And don't forget that phone feature on your phone! It is simple to schedule a call or spontaneously reach out rather than text and email.

Regardless of the setting, just don't forget to be thoughtful! Especially during tough times, be sure to avoid falling into conversations that in any way resemble the following: "You think that is a tough situation, wait till I tell you what is happening for me." It may be reflexive to try to relate to someone when they are sharing a negative experience, but this can unintentionally lessen what they are going through. Responding with: "Yes, I know . . ." can lead to frustration and a disconnect as well. Think back to a conversation you had with a friend or family member who is expressing their frustration with a situation happening in their life. Have you ever listened to someone vent about a situation, and responded with "Yes, I know how that feels . . ." when you have never actually experienced it yourself? Certainly not in the exact same way. You may instinctively be trying to show your understanding, but it can be very frustrating to the person who is sharing their story. It is much better to respond with, "That must be so frustrating" or "My heart goes out to you that you have so much on your plate."

If someone has chosen to share a negative or sensitive experience with you, it is important to not only listen to them, but acknowledge and thank them for choosing you as someone they are sharing this with. It is true that crises like COVID-19, mass shootings, and stock-market slumps cause worry and unease, but they can also promote a bond, because we actually have a conversation that shares a commonality. This is the time to let the people on the video chat or phone call know how much you appreciate them and how precious each interaction can be for you.

If you're disappointed that you're not getting these connections with people, you can help things along. Try encouraging your friend, family member, colleague, or customer to tell you more by using verbal cues to embolden them to continue to talk: "What is that like for you?," "What happened next?," "Hmmm . . ."

Some other ideas for cultivating connections now and in the future:

- Consider folks that may not be as active as you, an acquaintance, someone who supports the same charitable institution, or a neighbor you have not seen. Reach out to them, and better yet, make a schedule to reach out to one to two new people each week if you have the time. There is a great deal of loneliness in the

world, now more than ever. Be a friend and reach out
a hand via phone, email, or virtual communication.

- Many of your customers, restaurants where you
  dine, stores and services you support, and referral
  sources need Amazon, Yelp, and Trip Advisor
  reviews. They might write blog posts that
  welcome comments. Invest time in doing this and
  they will find a special place in their hearts just
  for you!

- Do your homework in order to remember
  something personal about people attending your
  board meeting or family reunion.

- Keep an informal database, especially with
  acquaintances. Or add notes to your contact.
  Do whatever works for you. Then, before you call
  or email, quickly scan your notes so you're up to
  speed.

Anyone reading this can be a leader and role model
supplying new techniques and innovative approaches to
staying in touch and cultivating connections, no matter
how tough times may be.

Whether you want to land a new job, cultivate connections during tough times, enhance your practice, gain listings, increase your billable hours, bring new people into your business or life, or make sure people remember you with referrals—pay attention to the feel-good factor. And enjoy the success that follows.

16

HOLIDAY PARTY SAVVY

Survive the holidays with grace. Every year we are faced with the inevitable holiday occasions. Holidays can mean the ideal family get-together or a day of awkward moments, uncomfortable silences, and eruptions of family feuds. Many we look forward to, some we are obligated to attend, and others our spouses drag us to.

Top Ten Holiday Table Conversation Land Mines

1. "Are you two ever going to get married?" Most of us mothers (I am guilty as charged!) along with the rest of the planet presume that longtime

dating results in marriage. It ain't necessarily so! And for those young people at the table already blissfully wed: "When are you two going to make me a grandmother?" Back off! If they wanted you to know their intimate intentions, they would be sure to send you a press release.

2. "I heard Erik got into Northwestern . . . Why in the world is he going to Michigan State instead?" Maybe the economy has put a damper on attending private institutions. Got a problem with the Spartans? Don't make assumptions about people, especially their finances.

3. "No, thanks. I gave up drinking after I saw the toll it took on you." This is meant to deliberately point a finger. If you must address someone's personal habits, do it in private! And making someone feel bad about him or herself does not typically motivate better behavior.

4. "Why did you two leave that beautiful home for this?" Inflation, pandemic, and job loss created a housing crisis for many, not just those strangers you read about in the newspapers. Remember what Mom always said: If you have nothing nice to say . . . shut up!

5. "I knew your candidate did not stand a chance. What do you have to say for yourself now?" Stop gloating, there are plenty people eating crow after the election, no need to rub it in. We are all in this together.

6. "Aren't you full yet?" or "Why aren't you eating anything?" Leave us alone about what we eat or don't eat and worry about what you put in your own mouth. Just because eating at the holiday dinner table is a marathon of gorging for some, for others it may be an Olympic feat of discipline. Also, just because you slaved over the pumpkin pie or prepared grandma's traditional stuffing does not mean we are required to consume it. Eating is a personal decision!

7. "Yes, I know you're a parent. But haven't you ever thought about working?" Whether someone chooses to work outside of the home or stay at home with their kids is their choice, and we should respect that choice and instead show a genuine interest in their life: "What are the challenges of staying at home with kids today?" or "Describe a typical day . . ." or "What keeps you busy outside of the kids?"

8. "I see you still can't be bothered with ironing a shirt." Leave him alone. His priorities are not the same as yours. Appreciate that he wore a nice button-down shirt!

9. "How is it that your son looks just like you and your daughter looks like she could be from a different family?" Personal questions that you do not know the answer to are never a good idea. Other examples include: "Did your son graduate?" and "How is the boyfriend?" "Did she go to prom?" and "Have you lost weight?"

10. "Did you cook this yourself, or did you just thaw it out?" You may be asking because you sincerely wish to know how you can create this dish yourself, but you are putting the host on the spot. Instead, ask for the recipe privately after the meal. If it was not homemade, she will let you know at that time or maybe be coy and say that the recipe is a family tradition that is not shared outside the family!

In general, don't be nosy, judgy, or presumptuous and stay out of any business that isn't your own!

Keep these cheat sheets in your breast pocket, on your device, or in your favorite cocktail purse.

Conversation Killers

1. *Are you married?* or *Do you have any kids?* Where are you going with either one of these if the response is "*no*"?
2. *How's your job at Boeing, United Airlines, Martha Stewart Enterprises, (fill in the blank)?* Unless you know the person well, assume nothing! Don't put them on the spot with those types of questions. Instead ask, *What's been going on with work?*
3. *How's your wife?* (She left, took all the money, the kids, and then got the house!)
4. *Merry Christmas! What are your Christmas plans?* Not everyone celebrates Christmas.
5. At all costs avoid *Is that real? Are those real?*

Top Ten Icebreakers for Holiday Parties

1. "What is your connection to the host/hostess or event?"

2. "What do you enjoy the most at this time/season of the year?"

3. "How does this season of the year affect your work?"

4. "Bring me up to date about your life/work/family since the last time we got together."

5. "Tell me about your plans for the holidays."

6. "Do you have a favorite holiday tradition?"

7. "What challenges do you encounter at this time of year?"

8. "Tell me about a special gift you have given or received."

9. "What is your favorite holiday? Why?"

10. "What do you have going on during the coming year?"

Meeting new people, spending time with family, and engaging in conversation with them can be exhausting and overwhelming. But it does not have to be this way. Skilled small talkers turn holiday gatherings into opportunities for success. In fact, they realize that these holiday functions are great for networking, reconnecting with family and friends, and (gasp!) meeting potentially interesting people.

Whether you are at a business meet-and-greet, a new boyfriend's family dinner, or a client's open house, you can use conversation skills as a tool to build new connections, while avoiding awkward pauses and uncomfortable conversations. After all, any relationship—business or social— starts with small talk.

17

CARPE DIEM

As we wrap up our conversation on small talk, I am reminded of the professor in *The Wizard of Oz* after his wizardry is discovered to be hocus-pocus. The erstwhile Wizard gives a provocative monologue when he tells the Lion, the Tin Man, and the Scarecrow that they already have what it is they've been seeking. All they need to do to be courageous, have a heart, or be intelligent is to claim their own skills. The Wizard merely bestows his good wishes formally.

You now have all my trade secrets right here. I have no more magic than you. You only need to continue practicing the skills, tips, and techniques demonstrated in this book. So, without further ado, I ceremoniously honor your newfound skills:

By the power vested in me as a former nerd who has transformed herself into a longtime successful Small Talker, I do hereby confer upon you the title of "Small Talker Extraordinaire." You are accorded all the rights, privileges, and responsibilities herewith. Let no party, gathering, group, or person intimidate you or squelch your conversational skills.

You are an officially competent conversationalist. Let go of any old labels you've given yourself that stand in the way of claiming conversation as one of your strengths. The tips and tricks enumerated throughout this book are commonsense solutions to everyday small-talking dilemmas. Only one requirement is essential to achieve small-talk excellence: practice. Over and over again I get confirmation about the value of small-talk skills. I hear about people whose lives have changed as dramatically as my own. A man in Florida got up the courage to ask a woman on a date, and now they're married. A woman in Ohio got promoted to head up the entire Midwest region for her company. A gentleman in his fifties in Colorado is building a new life after his wife died prematurely of cancer. She had always done all the talking for both of them.

Don't give up if you run into trouble. Calvin Coolidge once said, "Nothing in the world can take the place of persistence. Talent will not; nothing is more common than unsuccessful men of talent. Genius will not; unrewarded genius is almost a proverb. Education will not; the world is full of educated derelicts. Persistence and determination alone are omnipotent." Practice with your family and friends first, and as you gain confidence, move on to business associates and other people you regularly see.

Put yourself in social situations more frequently. Accept invitations. Join a trade organization, a volunteer group, or a club. At work, volunteer for projects that will allow you to work with different people. Small-talk opportunities abound when you find yourself with strangers who share a similar passion or occupation. During the next few weeks and months review the "Winning at Small Talk" worksheet on the following pages.

I hope you're truly winning at small talk. Fake it for a while till it becomes second nature. If you are diligent about practicing, you'll become an expert.

Winning at Small Talk

Please answer "yes" or "no" to the following questions:

1. I have joined or participated in at least one club or group activity in order to develop new business friendships or to meet new people.
2. I'm conscious of taking turns in most conversations so that I can learn more about others and help them get to know me.
3. I have used my contacts to help at least two people find new jobs, hook up with potential customers and clients, or go out on a date. I have provided information for other networking purposes.
4. I have attended at least two functions where I can meet people in my profession/industry or who are potential decision-makers or where I can make new friends or find romance.
5. If someone is friendly toward me it is easy to be friendly back. However, I don't wait to make sure someone is friendly before I am friendly toward him or her.

6. When someone asks me *What's new?*, instead of saying *Not much*, I often talk about something exciting in my life.

7. At meetings, parties, job fairs, and such, I introduce myself to people I don't know and come away knowing the names of at least three people.

8. During virtual meetings I jump in to say hello, not waiting to be formally introduced. Unless activity in my office or personal circumstances do not allow for a live video, I do not go dark. I demonstrate positive body language, good eye contact, and genuine interest.

ACKNOWLEDGMENTS

The need for additional funds drew my eye to a notice seeking a facilitator for a workshop on small talk at Colorado Free University, an enduring institution of life-long learning. No, it is not really "free." The cost to attend is low and the pay for teachers is minimal. Without any experience and no formal knowledge of my subject, I was hired to offer a workshop on small talk. I gained a great education. Attendees completed evaluations at the end of each workshop. These nuggets of information and critiques gave me gifts that keep on giving. These adult students from all walks of life described the skills and proficiencies they wished to learn and what they did not need or want to learn. They also taught me *how* they wanted to learn. Thousands of executives, salespeople, lawyers, engineers, bankers, and entry-level college grads passed through my classes at Colorado Free University and ultimately led me to the audiences I am in front of today. Students of conversation helped me develop *The Fine Art of Small Talk*, and for that I am thankful. I also appreciate our quest for lifelong learning.

Also, huge thanks to Hachette Books for recognizing the wonderful success of my original book, *The Fine Art of Small Talk*. And that since 2005, when it was first published, many conversation skills needed to be enhanced and updated. The newly revised second edition offers me a wonderful opportunity to serve readers around the world.

Also by
DEBRA FINE

Beyond Texting: The Fine Art of Face-to-Face Communication for Teenagers (Canon Publishers)

The Fine Art of the Big Talk: How to Win Clients, Deliver Great Presentations, and Solve Conflicts at Work (Hachette)

DebraFine.com